CW00406052

East Chesl... . .
North Staffs Ramble

Steve Saxton

Four Points Ramble Association

Published by the Four Points Ramble Association, 18, Bullfinch Walk, Manchester M21 7RG. www.fourpointsramble.org.uk

ISBN: 978-0-9555297-2-6

Printed and bound by: DeanPrint Ltd, Cheadle Heath Works, Stockport Road, Stockport SK3 0PR

Cover design by Pauline Gribben. The same drawing is seen in context on page 47.

The superb drawings and cartoons on pages 3, 13, 16, 21, 39, 75, 77, 94, 104, 111, 113, 135 & 141 are by Peter Field.

The maps and some other scruffy drawings are by the author.

Mary Ann's Waltz is by Ishbel Saxton. *Arthur's Walkabout, The Towpath,* the *Steamboat Waltz,* and *Umberto's Hornpipe* are by the author. All other tunes are traditional, apart from the hymn tunes. Chords and arrangements are supplied variously by Barbara Brown, Paul Maylor, Barbara Doyle, John Trigg, Ishbel Saxton, and the author.

The author is also grateful to Mr T. Richards, Miss C. Warrillow, and Mr W. Wain for permission to quote from the work of other writers.

Also available from the same author and publisher:

Four Points Ramble Book One: Ramble Through West Yorkshire.
Four Points Ramble Book Two: Ramble Past Manchester.

See the website www.fourpointsramble.org.uk for details of the beneficiary charities, which are different from this book.

GREYSTONES, LEEK

Contents

4

5

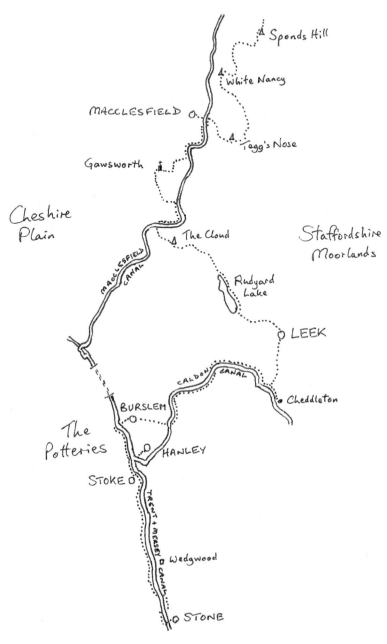

The route of this book

Introduction

This is a slow travel book, the third of a series describing a *potentially* continuous walk taking in the four extremities of England: the northernmost, southernmost, westernmost, and easternmost tips of the mainland. The book covers a 60-mile section of the journey south, taking in the East Cheshire and North Staffordshire hills and valleys, followed by the urban landscape of the Potteries.

The book is not intended as a trail guide. In some sections – for example when walking canalside – it is difficult to lose your way; and in others, such as where the Gritstone Trail or the Staffordshire Way are followed, good guides already exist. But where the reader could be unsure of the route being taken, some directions may be given.

The intention is to avoid unpleasant walking conditions, by and large; and to achieve a mixture of the remote and the familiar in the route, as well as a variety of walking between moderately strenuous and gentle, between the high places and the low.

As before, various interests will be indulged as opportunities arise: wildlife, history, literature, music, biography, industrial archaeology (in particular canals and railways in the age of steam), genealogy, heraldry, church history, topography and story-telling.

possible route

One: Sponds Hill to Tower Hill *(5 miles)*

Spikelets and awns – demolishing Cheshire – reprehensible cat – Arthur's Walkabout – demise of the Cheshire Hunt – Waulkmill Wood – Lovely Nancy – Saddle of Kerridge – The Rising Sun – woodnackers

12th July 2003

Almost a complete year after our last walk to the Bowstones, Ishbel and I returned, having walked most of the routes of Books 1 and 2 and some of this book in the intervening period. The weather was ideal for walking: sunny, but with a stiff cool breeze. The Gritstone Trail, broad and almost level, stretched along the ridge straight ahead of us towards Sponds Hill. According to the Trail Guide, this ridge track was a very old road, possibly dating back to prehistoric times. It made for good walking now, with views across the deep Todd Brook valley to the high Derbyshire hills on our left, and the Cheshire plain stretching away into haziness on our right.

When we came to the highest point of Sponds Hill, at 1347 feet, there was a flat metal plate engraved with the outlines of the surrounding hills and landmarks, so that Gritstone Trail walkers could identify all the peaks and tors. To the east across the valley was the steep wooded clough that contained Dunge Valley Gardens, a high west-facing collection of rhododendrons and similar upland plants that blazed with colour in the spring; we'd visited a couple of times and enjoyed the purple and red, white and gold, amid the green and red-brown of pines and hardwoods. The ridge above Dunge Valley stretched southwards, rising to Cat's Tor. The highest point, away to the South-East, was Shining Tor, surrounded by a cloud of hang-gliders like a gnat swarm. Walking on, my attention was divided between the panoramic views and the wild grasses at our feet. The trail guide said that the thin soil above the gritstone bedrock was only able to sustain coarse grasses such as Mat Grass and Wavy Hair Grass. Having (so far) no notion of what either of these grasses looked like, I had decided to take a couple of stems away to identify. Only when I started to look hard at the various flower-heads did I realise just how many different grasses were growing in quite a small area.

At home, later, I laid the little clutch of grass-stems out on the table, sorted them to eliminate duplicates, and used three wildlife books to try and identify the twelve different grasses that seemed to be represented. The book that gave the best background description of grass in general[1] expanded my vocabulary considerably, with the names of all the parts of the plant that might be distinguishing features: panicles, pedicles and auricles, spikelets, ligules and nodes, glumes and awns (what gorgeous words, and how wonderful still to find new words in one's mother tongue even in middle age); as well as the adjectives used to give some idea of shape: lance, wedge, ovate, and so on.

In the end I could only be tolerably certain of about half of the sample. Cocksfoot, *dactylis glomerata*, was easy, with its dense tufts and bird's claw shape;

---

[1] Cheatle, JRW (1976) *A Guide to the British Landscape* Collins

8

and so was Timothy Grass, *phleum pratense*, with its straight green cylindrical spike. I was also reasonably confident of the one-sided spike of Mat Grass, *nardus stricta* (left), and the long nodding fronds of Wavy Hair Grass, *deschampsia flexuosa*; especially since the Trail Guide had predicted them. Perennial Rye-Grass, *lolium perenne* (right), with alternating spike-lets either side of a wavy stem, seemed fairly safe, as did Yellow Oat-Grass, *trisetum flavescens*, where the spikelet with its bent awn helped identification.

But the other six grasses were harder to be certain of, and the following list is only a best guess:

- ❖ Purple Moor-Grass, *molinea caerulea*
- ❖ Sheep's Fescue, *festuca ovina*
- ❖ Red Fescue, *festuca rubra*
- ❖ Narrow-leaved Meadow-Grass, *poa augustifolia*
- ❖ Brown Bent Grass, *agrostis canina montana*
- ❖ Slender Fox-Tail, *alopecurus myosuroides*

I've listed the Latin names partly because they sound so beautifully exotic, but partly because the English names vary, and sometimes different books use different names. Does it really matter what they're called? They look the same, it might be argued, whatever the name; and indeed it seems a little obsessive to spread twelve types of grass out on a table and pore over books for ages trying to identify them. Is it not better just to appreciate the beauty of wild grasses?

In fact, having peered at, pored over, and tried to name different grasses, on the next walk I was noticing far more often than usual how beautiful the grasses were, whether they were identifiable or not. And it was also nice to recognise the ones I had got to know. Humans name things: it's in our nature, and has been since Eden. Children ask what things are called – until they lose their natural curiosity. Children, too, take an interest in objects that seem ordinary and nondescript to older people who have a more jaded appreciation of nature; it is well worth taking a closer look at familiar things to recapture a sense of wonder.

> The common things of earth are the most gracious gifts of God. None of us extract their full value, yet every man holds it in his power to make himself tenfold happier by a wise use of them. For true and continuous enjoyment of life is … found in the culture of love for common things, the untaxed game that no man can deprive us of, and which constitute the chief part of the beauties of the country.[1]

As we descended the southern ridge of Sponds Hill, the noise of a huge field full of hundreds of sheep grew gradually louder. The Trail Guide said that Brink Farm was stocked with Swaledale/Welsh Mountain crosses; but I didn't know how old the

---

[1] Grindon, LH (1882) *Country Rambles* Palmer & Howe: Manchester

leaflet was (bought for 39p from Chorlton Oxfam bookshop), and the farm could have restocked since. It didn't seem like a good plan to take twelve sheep home and lay them out on a table for identification: I might get into a bit of trouble from the farmer, and I would certainly get into a lot of trouble from Ishbel. So I contented myself with observation. In another field we saw two sheep with corkscrew horns that wound in two full circles, taking advantage of the shade under a monstrous yellow caterpillar-tracked vehicle. The monster's long muscular arm was extended as if contemplating activity; and in bold black letters on its rump was painted CHESHIRE DEMOLITION.

Well, where would you start if you wanted to demolish Cheshire? From this high vantage point we could see quite a lot of the county, and it was clear that demolishing it would be no easy task. But who had given the order to demolish Cheshire, anyway? Had Tony Blair finally lost the plot?

No no, said Ishbel, *this is one of Saddam Hussein's Weapons of Mass Destruction cunningly infiltrated onto English soil and ready to be deployed at 45 minutes notice.*

But it's not in disguise. It says it's going to demolish Cheshire.

Ah but – we have reliable intelligence from unimpeachable sources that Saddam Hussein has long been a master of the Double Bluff.

Good job Tony Blair helped George W Bush bomb Iraq to bits. There might have been hundreds of these fearsome machines. There might now just be a smoking hole where Cheshire used to be.

Political satire, and dodging speeding cars, occupied us along a hundred yards of Bakestonedale Road, until we found another waymarked stile beyond Brink Farm. The farm itself nestled in a saddle between two hills, substantial grey stone dwellings and long low barns that enclosed a yard packed with noisy sheep. The stile took us back into quiet pasture, and down towards an old stone quarry, now abandoned but still with odd bits of rusting machinery about. According to the Trail Guide, it opened as recently as 1900, and was known as the Klondyke Quarry because it produced golden stone.

On the ground it wasn't quite clear which way the Gritstone Trail now went: the map and guide agreed that it should pass to the left of the quarry, but there was no signpost and a clear track veering to the right of the quarry.[1] We decided to go with the map, and walked across the pathless meadow, dotted with thistles and clumps of Compact Rush, until we came to a small post with the Trail waymarker, a little black-and gold logo that could be heraldically blazoned as: *Or, a bootprint Sable, bearing a letter G of the first.*

14th July 2003

I returned alone, two days later. Ishbel was just starting back at work, but I had another week's freedom. I located the same waymarked post, near Klondyke Quarry, close to the small rise called Andrew's Knob.

---

[1] I should say that the Gritstone Trail was generally excellently waymarked. I walked more than half of it, and this was the only place more guidance would have been welcome.

I found, however, no sign of the erratic boulder that was described in the Trail Guide, and made my way steadily through the thickly thistled field towards a clump of trees. Two magpies rose chattering from the corpse of a sheep that was contorted into a pose worthy of Picasso's *Guernica*. A few paces on I passed downwind, briefly breathing in the stench of decomposition.

Magpies, nowadays, are so common that they are almost invisible, and I don't think I've mentioned any on the Four Points Ramble so far; I hardly notice them except at home when Arthur the cat used to bring one in. Unfortunately he usually neglected to kill his victim before bringing it in; having hauled it alive through the catflap, he liked to let it go and catch it again. Sometimes he did this while we were out; so it happened once that we arrived home after a long drive, ready for a cup of tea, to find: ornaments on the floor; the windowsills cleared of pot plants, which had scattered their earth over a wide area of carpet and cushions; little dabs of guano in various places; and, perched on the extractor fan in the kitchen (a spot beyond feline reach), a nervous but apparently uninjured magpie, which flew off when we opened the window.

Arthur came to us as a housewarming present, a neutered two-year old stray that friends of ours, who find homes for strays, were having difficulty placing (kittens are easier). We interviewed him and gave him an intelligence test; sadly, he cheated, managing to present his low cunning as true intelligence. He also succeeded in concealing his natural laziness, greed, deceitfulness and selfishness, as well as the fact that he was a bully, a coward, a thief and a vandal. The vet's notes, which I was once idly reading upside down (as you do), waiting for the credit card apparatus to finish muttering, included the word 'spiteful', scrawled in angry letters at the top of the card. As Ishbel said, if he hadn't been so cute he would soon have become a set of fiddle strings and a fur hat. She also warned him that she knew Korean students who had tempting recipes; but he remained incorrigible. To his credit it should be recorded that he might have had some sort of social conscience, for he used to visit several lonely old ladies and graciously allow them the satisfaction of feeding him titbits. I once wrote him a little tune, but he didn't like it, having no taste in music whatsoever.

Arthur's Walkabout

I emerged from the brief shade of a few trees into the sunshine of a cloudless day, and a fine view that stretched away into haziness. Closer, on the right, there were quarries visible across Bakestonedale, where, unsurprisingly, bakestones used to be made.

11

The map showed quarries away to the south as well; the whole area was scattered with a number of quarries, some of which yielded coal or clay for bricks or tiles, as well as stone.

Closer still, a Red Admiral posed on a clump of nettles – scarlet on black on dark green, one of innumerable perfect colour combinations to be seen in a country walk. A little further on, a Small Tortoiseshell posed likewise. Throughout the day there were many brown butterflies restlessly fluttering, always looking as if they were just about to settle and then changing their minds. Those that did pause long enough to identify all turned out to be Small Heaths.

The Trail continued gently downwards alongside a dry stone wall. Every now and again, sheep jammed into the narrow shadow thrown by the wall would twitch at my approach, then get painfully to their feet and lumber away, to stand and stare at me reproachfully until I had passed. Anyone not naturally hard-hearted would have been crippled with guilt by the time they arrived at the gate into the strip of woodland above Berristall Hall. Instead I enjoyed the view westwards, with the tower of Pott Shrigley church peeping from behind abundant trees.

The Shrigleys were local lords who lived in the old Berristall Hall; the present building dates from the 19th century, though it appears to have  been done up much more recently. The Trail descended steep grassy meadows below the Hall and entered another little wood near the valley floor, where I noticed the delicate near-white on green of the flowering grasses: probably Wood Millet, *milium effusum* (left), tallest and most open and finely-traced; Wood Meadow-Grass, *poa nemoralis* (right), shorter and smaller but also with loose and open pyramidal flower-cluster; and Creeping Soft-Grass, *holcus mollis*, with rather denser tufts of flowers. Whatever they were, when looked at carefully they were very beautiful.

Just below the wood the Trail crossed the Harrop Brook on a dinky little stone bridge: one span of a few feet and just a couple of feet above the water. I wondered at first if it was a modern construction; it looked almost like the sort of thing you see spanning a minuscule pond in a suburban garden. But apparently it was a genuine old packhorse bridge, recently renovated.

Beyond the bridge the Trail climbed a little, through more grassy, butterfly-rich fields, until it approached the Cheshire Hunt Inn, of which I had high hopes, since both the Trailwalker's Guide and the OS map marked it; and the day was hot and thirst-inducing. However a stone slab high on the wall was inscribed Cheshire Hunt Lodge AD 2001; and the immaculate stonework everywhere told the same story: the old pub had been converted to a dwelling.

PACKHORSE BRIDGE

Nearby was a tall estate agents' signboard with a red-lettered SOLD sticker plastered diagonally across. The adjacent stable block was empty, yet still in good order, awaiting its own renovation. On the end wall there was still a long green board: CHESHIRE HUNT INN FREE HOUSE.

Round the corner was a new-looking Country Café; but that was closed on Mondays. At least it would be open on other days, providing an oasis among all the ex-pubs no longer serving any kind of refreshment. Once you could find afternoon tea almost anywhere in the country, an arrangement that not only refreshed walkers but also provided welcome extra income for countryfolk, as the Victorian nature-lover Leo Grindon explains:

> ...there has sprung up a readiness on the part of country folks to open their doors in a hospitable spirit, which is quite tempting and delightful; and, most assuredly, nothing forms so pleasant a conclusion to an afternoon's ramble as to sit down in a neat cottage to a comfortable farmhouse meal, with its huge broad piles of bread and butter, and inexhaustible store of green salad and new-laid eggs. There, with the sun shining aslant through the old-fashioned window, the doors open, and the breeze gently peeping in, the cows lowing in the pasture, and the very atmosphere redolent of the country, we realise the fine hearty pleasurableness of a good appetite...[1]

In an adjacent field a tractor was turning hay to dry more quickly in the heat and drying breeze. I decided to have lunch at Oakenbank, not far ahead – I did have some food and water in case of need – and strode on along the short stretch of metalled road that the Gritstone Trail followed at this point. Down to the right could be seen the tall arch of Bollington Aqueduct, taking the Macclesfield Canal across a deep narrow valley; I had pleasant memories of both walking and cruising across, at different times. With the young people at our church, we several times hired a dayboat from a small boatyard in Higher Poynton; and once cruised southwards through Bollington.

---

[1] Grindon, *op cit*

On that occasion we'd added to the party a couple of Mongolian students; and they glowed all day with enjoyment of the space, and the hills, and the fresh air. They'd been stifling in the middle of Manchester for months, missing their native wide horizons.

The lane wound past Oakenbank, a cluster of old stone cottages, painstakingly restored and maintained, with immaculate gardens: every detail in place and carefully attended to. At the corner where the Gritstone Trail left the lane, tall trees shaded low stone walls, providing a cool and comfortable setting for sandwiches and water. The lane carried very little traffic; so the background music was birdsong and the wind in the treetops.

Refreshed, I followed the path steeply down, across a little stream, then steeply up again to Higher Ingersley, where a grassy track led past old stone farm buildings and out into more open pastureland. At a footpath junction the Gritstone Trail turned sharp right and began to descend again, with the grounds of the former Ingersley Hall on the right: built for John Gaskell in the 1770s, said the Trail guide. It was now known as Savio House, and seemed to be an educational establishment.

At the bottom of another steep descent, the Trail crossed the River Dean at Waulkmill, where there were industrial buildings to the right, down the valley towards Bollington; but the path led on and up another steep hill, through Waulkmill Wood, which is owned by the Woodland Trust. Waulkmill Wood is worth investigating; a little wandering and you'll find the tallest and straightest Scots Pine you ever saw, not to mention the biggest and stateliest beech.

Coming up out of the wood, the Trail wound around the north end of Kerridge Hill, giving panoramic views over Bollington Aqueduct again, and beyond that, the massive outline and tall brick chimney of Clarence Mill, built by the Swindells family (but there seems to be no connection with the Swindells in my own family tree – at least, if there is a connection, it must be before 1680). Swindells is a very local name: all Swindellses ultimately come from the *Swyn Delves*, or pig diggings, in the parish of Cheadle, less than ten miles away.

Clarence Mill was built in 1854, and according to Dennis Suleman, was famed for the fineness of its yarn, spun from Sea Island cotton and supplied to Nottingham for lace making.[1]

Halfway round the hill, the Gritstone Trail turned sharp left for a *really* steep ascent to the White Nancy tower; I took a deep breath and wondered whether to head straight up. On the map, however, a pub was marked just round the corner, and all this ascending and descending on a hot day makes one thirsty…

A little further on was the Redgate Tavern, which had clearly been a large and thriving establishment once, with an extensive beer garden, car park, and children's play area. But now it was empty, and a notice on the door explained that planning permission had been sought for conversion to two dwellings. This was right on the edge of Bollington, and somehow it looked as though there might be another pub just

[1] Suleman, D (1993) *On the Level* North Cheshire Cruising Club

TELESALES 0161 480 6571
brewery@frederic-robinson.co.uk
www.frederic-robinson.com

down around the corner. A brisk descent established that there was: the Red Bull, which was closed. It didn't seem wise to go right down into the middle of Bollington, since it would then be much further to climb back up to the top of the hill. In those days I didn't yet know the Dog & Partridge, with its excellent Robinson's bitter and Arthur Wakefield's friendly and fabulous Friday folk club. I turned thirstily and began the ascent.

Once at the top, a cool and pretty stiff east wind was a great relief, reducing overheating so that it was possible to enjoy the views: north towards Manchester; west across the Cheshire plain; and east to the Cheshire hill country, with the Derbyshire hills rising behind. White Nancy herself was a curious little solid beehive-shaped structure, said to have been built by the Gaskells of Ingersley to honour the victory at Waterloo.

> On the 18th day of June, me boys, eighteen hundred and fifteen,
> Both horse and foot they did advance; most glorious to be seen,
> Both horse and foot they did advance and the bugle-horn did blow
> And the sons of France were made to dance on the Plains of Waterloo.

The beehive wasn't always solid; there used to be benches under cover; but the vandalism had been such that the authorities bricked it up completely and painted it over – so now White Nancy was whiter than ever. The original Nancy, the lady that the monument was named for, was apparently one of the Gaskell family.

Lovely Nancy

Southwards from White Nancy was a long level ridge, the Saddle of Kerridge, with steep grassy slopes to the east, and extensive quarries to the left, which were still working: blocks of stone were piled here and there, the whirring of machinery could be heard, as well as the clear ringing dint of hammer on iron chisel.

16

All the way along the ridge the cool east wind made walking a pleasure; in several spots there were patches of the most beautiful red-stemmed grass, with delicate silver pedicles waving in the wind, giving a wonderful ripple effect in the larger patches. The grass looked so distinctive that I didn't take a sample, thinking it would be easy to identify; but none of the books mentioned those vivid red stems. The least unlikely possibility was Silvery Hair-Grass, *aira caryophyllea.*

Coming towards me was a figure who was clearly an experienced walker: stocky and fit-looking with short silver hair, he was carrying a map in a sensible plastic case. We exchanged greetings; then I was looking for the spot where the Gritstone Trail left the ridge and descended south-eastwards. It's clear enough, when you actually get there. The path slanted gently downwards: according to the Guide, this was the path the Kerridge quarry workers who lived in Rainow used on their way to work. Rainow

was very clearly visible on the opposite hillside, compactly laid out with the chapel on the left and the church on the right.

Checking the map, I found the descent should steepen; and this brought me down to a lush area of longer grass – Cocksfoot (right) and Timothy grass (left) amongst it – and then under trees near the bottom of the valley. The guide had a photograph of the ruins of Cow Lane Mill, but there was nothing to be seen except a couple of rabbits scuttering about under the trees. Down here was sheltered from the east wind, and it was hot walking once I emerged from the trees, crossed the stream, and began the short ascent to the road at Tower Hill. The line of houses on the road all had trim back gardens; from one came the song of a canary. Just along the road was the Rising Sun, which had some wonderful flowers in the garden … but was closed. If it had been open, it might well have been worth commemorating with the following stirring hornpipe:

The Rising Sun

17

4th April 2007

Nearly four years later Ishbel and I returned to Tower Hill to walk back to the Saddle and enjoy the clear early spring air. This time the ruins of Cow Lane Mill were quite obvious; I couldn't have paid much attention when I walked past before, though there would have been much more undergrowth in high summer. The drumming of woodpeckers echoed persistently around the valley; after a while, we could be fairly sure that there were three distinct sources. Nevertheless it was some time before we finally saw one: and then there were three, high in the bare branches of tall birches.

They moved closer, and we were able to watch them scuttling along and around branches with the 'easy adroitness' described by the Reverend Francis Morris.[1] The vivid scarlet of the undertail patch and the big white patches on the wings identified them as Greater Spotted Woodpeckers, *dendrocopos major* according to Linnaeus; though Morris makes the Latin name *picus major*, and notes that they may also be known as Whitwalls, Woodwalls, Woodnackers, or Woodpies. According to Thorburn,[2] they breed all over the Old World, from the Canaries to Kamchatka, and are not in any sense a rare bird in England; yet we'd never had such a clear and extended opportunity to observe them.

Kerridge Hill

[1] Morris, Rev FO (1850) *British Birds*
[2] Fisher, J (1967) *Thorburn's Birds* Ebury Press

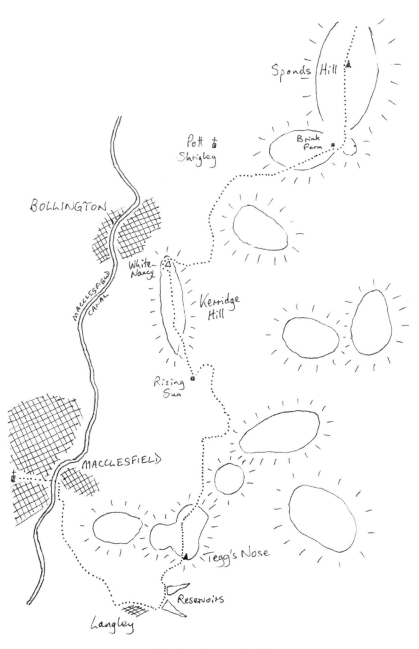

Map for chapters 1 & 2

Two: Tower Hill to Macclesfield *(5 miles)*

Jaw crusher – Umberto – Greenall's – a bishop confounded – pub with Aspect – no welcome for Bonnie Prince Charlie – death of a spy – leather software – grubby cheque – Poverty Knock

15th July 2003

I returned to the Rising Sun by bus, ready to continue the walk from Tower Hill. A phone call to a bus information number had elicited the advice to take a number 60 towards Lyme Park; in fact what was needed was a 62 to New Mills, which stopped near the Rising Sun. Fortunately I had got hold of the right information before getting on the wrong bus. After a hundred yards' walk along the road, at the corner the Gritstone Trail turned off right, up a lane, then right again on a path. Where the path branched off was a newly landscaped area with a bench, proudly proclaiming 'This seat and the oak tree were placed here by Rainow Women's Institute to celebrate the millennium'.

Although I'd hardly warmed up, much less needed a rest, it seemed a shame not to sample the WI bench; the view was so lovely: sharply-defined slopes and steep valleys coloured in every shade of green and yellow, scattered with livestock, dotted with trees and stone houses and lined with stone walls, leading the eye up to the tall hills, Big Low and Yearns Low prominent; and over all, a blue sky delicately brushed with soft wisps of cloud. 'Meal-drift', Hopkins called clouds like that[1], meaning like the patterns seen at a cornmill, where the lightest and finest flour is blown about the floor by a soft draught. It was the sort of view you really want in the middle or at the end of a walk. At the beginning, it made one wonder what was the point of walking – why not just sit and enjoy the view? And why not leave it to the floriloquent Grindon to describe it?

> No description can convey a perfect idea of the loveliness of this part of the walk... The long-extended survey of hill and dale, the innumerable trees, clothing the slopes at agreeable distances with the most picturesque of little woodlands, bright and cheerful in their unsullied raiment of leaves that are only yet learning the sweetness of sunshine; the rise and fall of the ground; the incessant turns and sinuosities of the pathway, every separate item is a treat...[2]

Still, eventually I stirred myself, and headed up the path towards Gorsey Brow, to be rewarded by the sight of a falcon perched on a bare branch at the top of a pine tree that seemed to be about a third dead. The Trail sloped on upwards through open country; here and there were Small Heath butterflies. Ahead was the bulk of Ely Brow, maybe three hundred feet above, but it wasn't necessary to climb it; the Trail turned right and came to the edge of a deep winding clough. A signpost directed trailwalkers over a stile and then steeply down to the bottom of the clough, over the stream and up Bull Hill on the other side.

---

[1] *Hurrahing in Harvest*, Gerard Manley Hopkins.

[2] Grindon, *op cit*

As I followed the path up Bull Hill, the air was full of swooping, squeaking martins, flocking round a nearby barn. A stile led to a main road: the A537 Macclesfield to Buxton, once considered the most dangerous in Britain. Because of its sharp bends and changes of gradient, interspersed with fast straights, it was a favourite playground of bikers – particularly middle-aged bikers returning to two wheels after years of boring family cars. But the police and other traffic authorities had tackled the problem with a 50mph limit and increased patrols, and they were justly proud of their success. As a result of their sterling efforts, the A537 was now only the *second* most dangerous road in Britain – though since the new most dangerous was in the north of Scotland, this Macclesfield to Buxton bikers' paradise was still the most dangerous in England. It was worth being extra cautious in crossing diagonally to the steps in the stone wall opposite.

Once safely beyond the road, the path led on, steadily upwards on a long slope of rough grassland. Eventually it levelled out at around 1200 feet and began to descend towards the aptly-named Windyway House. Just beyond the house, on the same high windy saddle, was the car park and information centre for Tegg's Nose Country Park, with a picnic area giving superb views to the south and east. I sat in the shade of a small rowan, for the sun was hot, and ate some sandwiches, watching the swifts skimming high above. Far higher still was the silhouette of a buzzard, slowly wheeling on a thermal.

The information centre carried a plaque saying that the Gritstone Trail had been formally opened by county councillor J.H. Godwin on 6th August 1978, which, as I read it, was just under 25 years before. How does a Trail celebrate a Silver Jubilee, I wondered, as I followed the Country Park's trail towards the Quarry Exhibition.

The Exhibition turned out to be fearsome large-scale machinery: Butters Derrick Crane, for example, or the Swing Saw, with six blades, which used diamond grit to help cut through the stone, and sounded like something out of Edgar Allen Poe. Most frightening was the Jaw Crusher (don't even try to imagine it) which could crush 100 tons of stone a day. So that's why you only hear about Tegg's Nose, and his Jaw is never mentioned...

While focusing on the machinery, I caught a flash of blue falcon – peregrine? – but not a clear enough sight to be sure. From the quarry the Trail wound round the brow of the hill before plunging suddenly down a long open slope. The descent brought an ever-changing perspective on the surrounding country, as various features became more prominent once seen from below. Eventually the path ran under the shade of oak, beech and hornbeam trees, ending in some steps down to Teggsnose Reservoir. After 400 feet of thigh-stressing rapid descent, it was a relief to be on the level, if only briefly.

At the far end of the dam, I left the Gritstone Trail and took the road down into Langley village. The Trail had been exhilarating walking in its nine miles so far; though sometimes thirsty work, as I'd passed two ex-pubs, two closed pubs and a closed café; and nothing at all open. Still, today I would be all right, as I was going right through Langley. Such optimism: it was soon deflated when St Dunstan's Inn came into sight, looking ever closeder as I came closer. A notice on the door gave the opening times: not before 7.30pm except on Sundays. As I stared at the heavy black iron-studded door, the heat seemed to intensify; here there was none of the cooling breeze which had made Tegg's Nose so pleasant.

Nothing for it but to keep going. A little further down the street, through the open door of a repair garage could be seen a magnificent 1920s-style open tourer: all brass and rich red paintwork, with the name 'Simplos' atop the bull-nose radiator. I found myself peering in at the doorway – the workshop was deserted – but I didn't quite have the cheek to go right in.

Just after Langley Hall, a signpost showed where the footpath to Macclesfield headed off to the right. I followed it across a meadow containing some big grey cows, down to the River Bollin, over a footbridge and up the other slope. The heat increased as I headed up towards Birch Knoll and then followed the path round the flank of the hill. Approaching Macclesfield, the path entered a golf course and ran under the very welcome shade of some hawthorns. A vivid orange butterfly with black spots posed on a nettle. Following the map very closely, I turned left into an extremely narrow alleyway between high walls: not a place for claustrophobics, nor for prop forwards, who would have jammed sideways.

The alleyway came out on a dirt track, with a few parked cars; among them, two old Fiat Pandas, which awakened nostalgic memories of the little grey 4x4 Panda we ran from 1987 to 1996. His name was Umberto, and he took us to Turkey, round Turkey for six months, and back again; to Sweden four times, with excursions all round Sweden, as well as into Norway, Denmark, and Germany; to Hungary and back twice; and many times to and from Scotland. He had 11,000 miles on the clock when we bought him, and 10,000 on the clock when we sold him, with a valid MOT and still going strong. By that time Umberto contained parts of at least four other Pandas; but he was still a reliable little car in that he always broke down close to home, and never stranded us anywhere.

Umberto's Hornpipe

Another left turn, over the canal and round a couple of corners was the Beehive, a pub which was actually open. The name of the pub might well have been a reference to the arms of Roe, a family of distinction in Macclesfield since the days of Edward III: *Argent, a hive and bees flying thereabout Sable.* Inside, the  Beehive was very dark after the brilliant sun outside; there were ceiling fans stirring the warm air; brass rails top and bottom of the bar gleamed in the gloom. It was an old-fashioned boozer, full of unashamed unreconstructed bad taste. I puzzled the barman by ordering an orange squash as well as a beer, since there was clearly only one of me. The squash went down so fast I hardly tasted it (that was why I ordered it – I wanted to taste the beer), and before I started the Greenall's I was startled by the huge drops of sweat that sprang out on my forearms. So it really had been hot out there.

The Greenall's was rather nice: dry and yet quenching. This former Warrington brewer had been swallowed up by Scottish and Newcastle; but the real ale buffs hadn't particularly rated Greenall's before the takeover, and some said that when cask ale production was switched to Tetley's in Leeds the beer sold under the Greenall's label improved no end. Others even suggested that it *was* Tetley's, with only the clip on the handpump being Greenall's.

From the Beehive it was a short step back to Bridge 40, and onto the towpath, and now I had linked up with the next section of the walk which we had done seven months before. Then there had been ice on the canal, and now it was baking hot. Among the moored boats were pleasant names, as always: *Tranquillity* and *Zephyr* were two that caught the eye. Just by the bridge were *Speckled Hen* and *Glayva*, both of which I had last seen in Skipton the previous September. Other long-distance travellers were *Liberty* from Great Haywood, away south on the Trent & Mersey (we'll pass there on this walk eventually) and *Elizabeth Nelson* from Birmingham.

20th December 2002

Looking for a decent pub lunch in Macclesfield ('Where shall we have lunch?' very much the Sophistication stage of civilisation), Ishbel and I were walking round in circles after having driven round in circles. We were beginning to fear a regression to the Survival stage ('How shall we eat?'); at one point we found ourselves climbing the 108 Steps, which were steep enough to make at least one of us grumble. I had read of the enterprising Macclesfield motorist who drove down these steps in the 1920s, and thought nothing much of it; seeing the steps now, feeling the steepness and the tug of gravity, it was obvious he must have been a complete lunatic.

At the top of the steps was St Michael's, where two of my ancestors were married during the Commonwealth. The details are recorded in the parish register of Gawsworth, but that charge was possibly vacant at the time, and so the mayor of Macclesfield married Thomas Braddock and Elizabeth Gardner:

23

Descendants of Thomas Braddock

Thomas Braddock b: 1628 Bosley = **Elizabeth Gardner** m. January 13, 1656/57 MacClesfield

James Braddock b: 1661 Gawsworth = **Jane Whitlock** m. June 06,1695 Prestbury

John Braddock b: 1714 = **Mary Shaw** b: 1720 Gawsworth m. April 19,1747 Gawsworth

- **Elizabeth Braddock** b: 1747
- **Samuel Braddock** b: 1750 Gawsworth = **Martha Knight** b: 1746 Marton by Congleton m. July 27,1774 Prestbury
  - **John Braddock** b: May 30,1780 Gawsworth
  - **William Braddock** b: July 17,1784 Gawsworth = **Charlotte Hibbert** b: 1784 Ashton under Lyne m. April 13,1804 Stockport
    - **Samuel Braddock** b: 1777
    - **Samuel Braddock** b: 1816 Ashton under Lyne
    - **Edward Linney** b: 1807 Ashton under Lyne m. June 16,1832 Manchester Cathedral = **Judith Braddock** b: 1814 Ashton under Lyne
    - **William Braddock** b: 1819 Ashton under Lyne
    - **Betty Braddock** b: 1786
    - **Thomas Braddock** b: 1788
    - **George Braddock** b: 1790
- **John Braddock** b: 1756 Gawsworth
- **John Braddock** b: 1758
- **Hannah Braddock** b: 1760
- **William Braddock** b: 1765

Bottom generation:
- **Hannah Braddock** b: 1804 Ashton under Lyne
- **John Braddock** b: 1807 Ashton under Lyne
- **Nancy Braddock** b: 1809 Ashton under Lyne
- **Thomas Braddock** b: 1819 Ashton under Lyne
- **James Braddock** b: 1822 Ashton under Lyne
- **Alfred Braddock** b: 1827 Ashton under Lyne
- **Henry Braddock** b: 1829 Ashton under Lyne

13 Jan 1656 Thomas Braddocke of this parish son of John Braddocke of Boseley, and Elizabeth Gardner of Sutton daughter of Francis Gardner of Winckle in the parish of Prestbury, published Dec 28th, Jan 4th, & 11th, married at Maxefeild by Mr. Wm Rowe, maior of Maxefeild.

The Commonwealth period is an unusual one for family historians, for records tend to be either fuller than at other periods, as above, or non-existent. Thomas Braddock was the great-great-great-grandfather of Judith Braddock (my great-great-great-grandmother), whose early death was described in Chapter 8 of Book 2. A tree is given opposite.

St Michael's, Macclesfield is also where a certain David Simpson was acting curate in the 1770s. The bishop suspected him of Methodism – with reason, Simpson's evangelical views were not secret – and refused to confirm the appointment as curate. Charles Roe, a local industrialist, was sympathetic, as was his brother James Roe, Simpson's vicar. The upshot was that Charles Roe arranged for the building of a new church specifically for Simpson to preach in: Christ Church, with a particularly tall tower so that, although the new church stood on lower ground, the top of the tower was level with the top of St Michael's – one in the eye for the bishop.

A selfless and costly action on Charles Roe's part? Perhaps, at first; but he managed to arrange the terms of the Act authorising the new church so that he retained the right to sell space for graves and vaults in the graveyard: a profitable long-term investment. At any rate, Simpson preached there till his death a quarter of a century later; so the bishop's obduracy had anything but the effect intended.

On the tower of St Michael's were various coats of arms; one that caught the eye was Sutton, blazoned *Argent, a chevron between three blowing horns Sable*, which were actually the arms of the Forest of Macclesfield, alluding to the earlier and simpler arms of Delamere forest: *Argent a blowing horn Sable*. Another was Fitton, a family we would meet again in Gawsworth: *Argent, a bend Azure charged with three garbs Or.*

Lunch still eluded us, and we might soon have been reduced to the extremity of the Hon John Byng (right), who came to Macclesfield in 1792 and 'was happy to attack a boiled Buttock of a bull' – as he added wryly, 'hunger is not refined'.[1] Round the corner, we thought we had found somewhere, until at the last moment we saw the sign forbidding trainers on the feet of those who wished to enter that superior pub, which will not be named here. They deserve no publicity. Fortunately not far away was the Bate Hall, a late 16th century building ...

---

[1] Andrews CB ed (1934) *The Torrington Diaries* Eyre & Spottiswoode

- which had been a pub for more than 200 years
- which didn't concern itself with customers' footwear
- which had food
- which served Marston's
- and which had what Chris Parker would call Aspect.

Aspect, in Parkerspeak, is hard to define, but you know it when you see it. In this case part of the Aspect was decoration which was not only tasteful but interesting. The beef and ale pie helped, too. We were actually sitting in a modern extension to the old pub, but we nonetheless felt a sense of history, of a long and eventful past. In the days of Edward the Confessor, Macclesfield had been held by the Saxon Earl Edwin, and valued at eight pounds; by the time of Domesday, the land then held by the Norman Hugh Lupus was worth only twenty shillings: a stark economic reminder of the devastation and misery caused by the Conqueror's Harrying of the North.

One of Macclesfield's later moments of excitement was in 1745, when they realised that Bonny Prince Charlie's army was in Manchester, only a few miles distant. The locals chose one Sampson Salt to go as a spy to Stockport and find out which way the rebel army was headed. Hearing nothing, they assumed that for the moment all was well; but in fact Sampson had been captured, and so they had little warning before the advance guard came riding into Macclesfield. An eye-witness[1] reported on the reappearance of Sampson Salt:

> Immediately afterwards came in a regiment of horse…said to be commanded by the Duke of Perth and [in] the 2nd or 3rd rank was the poor fellow (our Clyent Sampson Salt by name) who had been sent out as a Spy, Guarded by four terrible fellows with their Drawn Swordes. They soon found he was a townsman and that the Eyes of the Inhabitants were upon him. But fear had so metamorphosed our friend that his neighbours scarcely knew him: he was shorter by half a yard at least than the day before. If he cast an eye right Damn you, says a ruffian, you must not look that way. If he lookt to the left, Damn you don't look that way, so he was forst to conduct his two eyes directly betwixt the two ears of his Palfry – and the while the Guards kept laughing and pointing at him and to the people who beheld his distress.

The Prince's entourage had high hopes of a good reception, after their success at Manchester, but they were met with stony faces and silence. Manchester, then as now, had been radical and ready for alternatives; Macclesfield, then as now, was conservative, preferring the status quo, and distrusting anyone wanting to change it. Reluctantly the townsfolk gave up arms, cash, provisions; and the bakers worked overtime, and then some, to provide bread for an army which, at about 6000, was double the population of the town. The soldiers were relatively well-behaved, and few locals were harmed at this stage.

It seems that soon after the army left Macclesfield on the way south, Sampson Salt was either released or contrived to escape.

---

[1] John Stafford, a local lawyer

He fled southwards to Stone, where he found part of the Hanoverian army; however, being 'frightened out of what little sense he had', he failed to communicate the true situation, and was this time suspected of being a Jacobite spy, and imprisoned again. Eventually released, he made his trembling way back to Macclesfield just in time to hear that the returning rebels were about to re-enter the town. The stress of hearing this presumably brought on a heart attack, because he is said to have collapsed and died on the spot.

A lot of other Macclesfield folk were not very happy to see the Prince and his army again, having meanwhile committed themselves to the government cause by raising money for the defence of the realm. The Mayor and half the town fled, leaving the town 'very thin of Inhabitants and very dismal were the countenances of those who were left in it. The only comfort...to find the Rebels lookt full as dismal themselves.'

Not only dismal, but very angry. Having been encouraged at Manchester, they were now retreating solely because they had found so little support among the English since then. Macclesfield, which had watched them go by in sullen silence, and then subscribed to help them be defeated, symbolised their rejection and impending defeat. The Jacobites threatened the Lady Mayoress with fire and sword if she did not hand over the list of subscribers, then used the list to make each subscriber pay an equal amount, or have his house burnt down. Most paid.

The Duke of Cumberland, and the pursuing Ha-noverian army, were the next to arrive, posing the folk of Macclesfield two problems. Firstly, they had to persuade Cumberland that they had only paid money to the rebels under extreme duress; secondly (greatly daring) to suggest that since they had now paid huge amounts of money *twice*, could they perhaps have a refund? or perhaps a discount on the next tax bill? or something?

Apparently Cumberland (right) was not totally unsympathetic. No doubt he promised to give the matter his earnest consideration at the earliest opportunity.

Once the second army had finally departed, Macclesfield could get on with making money; and for the next 200 years, that meant silk. Charles Roe had opened the first silk mill just two years before the rebellion; and soon many others were set up in competition, and the population expanded considerably. Most of the mills are long gone, but some idea of the process of silk weaving, and the importance of the industry to Macclesfield, can be gained at the silk museum at Paradise Mill.

We had visited Paradise Mill a couple of years earlier with Ishbel's mother on a horrible wet afternoon. The museum can be thoroughly recommended as a place to take mothers-in-law, who will find it fascinating; in fact we all found it fascinating. We were particularly intrigued by the Jacquard system of machine control, which determined the pattern of weave by means of holes punched (or not punched) in strips

27

strips of leather – a binary system which was actually a simple computer, long before Babbage or Turing tackled the idea. Leather software, and wooden hardware (left); and probably more reliable than what I'm sitting in front of just now. When will Past Times start selling replicas?

'Silk Town', Macclesfield was called, and the local football team are still the Silkmen; but in the 20th century it gained another name: 'Stickytown' or 'Treacletown'. In 1900 a barrel of treacle rolled off a cart in Beech Lane and burst: the contents flowed down Hibel Road, and the locals gathered what they could as best they could. It made an absolute paradise for the children, who soon became almost unbelievably sticky.

In the heyday of silk manufacture, some of the entrepreneurs were so successful that they opened their own banks. As we sat, replete with beef and ale pie, in the Bate Hall, browsing in the Town Trail, we saw that the Brocklehursts' Old Bank Building was just around the corner in King Edward Street. Heading out for a quick stroll, we not only found the bank, but round another corner saw Jordangate House, where John Brocklehurst had lived. A firm of architects now occupied the ground floor, while the upper floors looked rather in need of their professional help to make good some dilapidation.

The power, even majesty, of these local banker/magnates is shown in the story told by Harold Whiston, then a young man working for one of Brocklehurst's clients, who were owed quite a lot of money. Young Harold was sent to ask for some payment:

> I was shown up to the great man's office, where he sat in state with his cashier. 'Well, young man, what brings you here this morning?' I replied timidly, 'My father sent me down to see if we could have some money'. 'Money', said Brocklehurst, 'do we owe you any?' and turning to his cashier he asked, 'What do we owe them at Langley this morning?' The cashier turned to the ledger and replied, '£5,200, sir'. 'Do we, by Jove,' said the old gentleman and taking a rather dirty envelope from his desk he wrote 'Pay Bearer £5,200 W.C.B.'[1]

To young Harold's amazement, the cheque was honoured by the bank. We may have been taught that a cheque can in theory be written on anything, but most of us would still be sceptical in practice, especially if the amount was so high (difficult to calculate, but the current equivalent might be half a million or more). 'Good lad,' said his father when Harold came back with the money, 'I'll send you again.'

Another member of a Macclesfield banking family was Bishop JC Ryle, who grew up here in luxury and privilege, captained Eton and Oxford at cricket, and

[1] cited in Davies, CS (1961) *A History of Macclesfield* Manchester University Press

by his own admission never read a word of the Bible from the age of seven until he was twenty-one. At that stage a very serious illness brought him up short, and he became a Christian; yet it was not until his father's bankruptcy, a few years later, that Ryle's pride was finally broken. Everything was gone: his horses, his dog, his home; everything he cared for, and he eventually gave himself completely to God's service.

> [A man] must cast away all pride and high thoughts, and conceit of his own goodness. He must be content to go to heaven as a poor sinner saved only by free grace, and owing all to the merit and righteousness of another…
> Now this sounds hard to some. I do not wonder. 'Sir,' said a godly ploughman to … Hervey of Weston Favell, 'it is harder to deny proud self than sinful self. But it is absolutely necessary.'[1]

Not so much of Macclesfield's silk money found its way to the actual weavers, who formed unions to try and keep wages up. The hand-loom weavers of Macclesfield have a claim to be the oldest trade union in the country, for as soon as the Combination Act was repealed in 1826 they set up the association which became the Macclesfield Handloom Weavers Association. It had limited success in keeping wages high, but at least hand-loom weaving persisted in the town for over a century after power looms were first introduced. In hard times the Association were irreverently known as the Poverty Knockers Union, after the old song:

Macclesfield made money out of silk; but the trade did not bring benefits to all. Wending our way back through the town centre, we remembered the report cited by Engels (right) in 1845:

> It is evident, at a glance, whence the distortions of these cripples come; they all look exactly alike. The knees are bent inward and backwards, the ankles deformed and thick, and the spinal column often bent forwards or to one side. But the crown belongs to the philanthropic manufacturers of the Macclesfield silk district. They employed the youngest children of all, even from five to six years of age.

---

[1] Ryle, JC (1879) *Holiness*

29

In the supplementary testimony of Commissioner Tufnell, I find the statement of a certain factory manager Wright, both of whose sisters were most shamefully crippled, and who had once counted the cripples in several streets, some of them the cleanest and neatest streets of Macclesfield. He found in Townley Street ten, George Street five, Charlotte Street four, Watercots fifteen, Bank Top three, Lord Street seven, Mill Lane twelve, Great George Street two, in the workhouse two, Park Green one, Peckford Street two, whose families all unanimously declared that the cripples had become such in consequence of overwork in the silk-twisting mills. One boy is mentioned so crippled as not to be able to go upstairs, and girls deformed in back and hips.

The misery of the early years of the industrial revolution had parallels in earlier times. There was plague here in 1603, and a hundred and thirty died. Some streets were worse hit than others; standing at the market cross, we can see Chestergate, where 8 died; Mill Street, where 10 died; and Church Street, where only one died. Did the folk of Church Street just have good immunity, we wondered as we turned aside to descend the 108 steps again, or were they more prosperous and less flea-ridden?

From the bottom of the 108 Steps, a brisk walk under the railway, past the Arrighi Bianchi furniture shop with its wonderful glass frontage, and up the Buxton Road brought us to the Macclesfield Canal.

Three: Macclesfield to Gawsworth *(4 miles)*

Muscle-making Strength of Man – mallard on ice – snake bridge – serious training – Brindley's apprenticeship – Banks's marketing – skew bridge design – Jubilee – tulgy wood – concerned and thoughtful spaniel – kissing gates – writhen roots

20ᵗʰ December 2002

On a cold and cloudy day near Christmas, Ishbel and I set out from Buxton Road Bridge on the canal to stretch our legs and work up an appetite for lunch. The first thing we noticed was two fine stone arches low in the wall of the Puss in Boots pub; it was difficult to guess for certain what purpose they once served. Perhaps beer had been delivered by water, and the barrels could be rolled up the slight slope and straight into the cellars?

Ahead was the bulk of Hovis Mill, where a hundred years ago flour was ground in the distinctive Hovis way for distribution to franchise bakers. Hovis was short for *hominis vis*, that is, the Strength of Man, and was persuasively marketed by Fitton & Son, who had bought the patent from a Staffordshire baker:

> When striving to KEEP THE WOLF FROM THE DOOR, remember that it is not always the cheapest that is the most economic, but the vast superiority of HOVIS over any other bread, either brown or white, both in its bone and muscle making substances, secures for it the coveted position of the "CHEAPEST and BEST."

The recipe for Hovis involved adding treated wheatgerm to white flour, and was one of many Victorian initiatives to encourage the masses to eat something healthier than white bread; local bakers in those days often could not produce a wholemeal loaf that was tasty enough to tempt the customer. Hovis was smoother in texture and less sour than the typical wholemeal or wheatmeal bread of those days.

The Hovis Mill was now immaculately restored and converted to dwellings; the old chimney stood proudly above, and an assortment of narrowboats were moored below: *Charlotte, Marianne,* and *Charlotte Emma; Jaywalker* and *Voyager; Snafu* and *Tir nan Og; Blue Heron* and *Blue Mist* – all fairly typical of narrowboat names. A smart cruiser was named *John Rennie*; logical to commemorate a canal engineer. More surprising was *Sir Daniel Gooch*, the Great Western Railway engineer, rather out of his territory here in the north (though perhaps the boatowners knew that he had worked on the Leeds & Manchester Railway). *John Lee Hooker* is not a name you instantly associate with canals either: presumably this was an owner with at least two separate enthusiasms.

Here in the shadow of the great mill there had been a revival in canal activity in the early fifties; one of the first IWA national rallies was held here in 1953. Soon afterwards the Wyvern Shipping Co was established by Lord Geoffrey Percy, using the narrowboats *Benevolence, Duchess of York, Victoria,* and *Duchess of Athol.* Unfortunately the company found soon afterwards that the Macclesfield Canal had become too shallow for economically viable loads to be carried , and the boats

31

were transferred elsewhere. It made a sad postscript to the story of an area that had once been a centre of freight forwarding: Pickford's used to have a considerable fleet of boats based here, with daily fly boats to Wolverhampton, Birmingham, and London.

Beyond the moorings was a British Waterways maintenance yard; it was reassuring to see, alongside the sections of concrete culvert pipe, a fair quantity of quarried and squared stone for repairs to stone-built structures. Opposite, a neat white house fronted onto the towpath, suggesting that it had had a canal function once. Further on, Great Tits squeaked among the bare branches of bushes above the wall; and squirrels scuttled along the wall, then flung themselves up, down, along and around the branches, paused, scratched themselves, wrinkled their noses and generally looked cute. They may just have been rats with good PR, but they were fun to watch.

Across the canal was a terrace of newish houses built to make the most of the canal frontage (well, backage, really); the owners clearly appreciated that aspect and had laid out their back yards sympathetically. A swan floated serenely towards us, hoping perhaps for bread. It had a large green ring on one leg; we wondered who was keeping count, and of what – all the swans on the canal? or in Cheshire? in England?

Ahead was Holland's Bridge; a simple canal bridge, but the stonework was wonderful, and the curve of the arch, curling slightly inwards at the bottom to suggest a pure oval, was immensely satisfying to the eye. The air, however, was too cold to stand and admire for more than a moment. We pressed on, and as we got further from the town, we saw evidence of what our fingers and ears were telling us – it was almost freezing. On the towpath some puddles had a skin of ice, usually broken by previous walkers; and thin angular sheets of ice were floating on the canal. Among the sheets of ice slightly thicker shards from an earlier freeze stood an inch or so proud.

We came across a couple of dozen mallard, some paddling in the clear water, others walking skiddily on the ice, and some falling through the thinnest pieces. It looked cold fun to me, but Ishbel said their feet don't feel the cold. I hoped she was right. It was a good morning for birds, though we saw nothing unusual. Flocks of sparrows cheeped in the hawthorns; ever since we heard that their numbers were dwindling we had taken a bit more notice of sparrows; they were enthusiastic and cheerful birds, and really quite handsome. A chaffinch gave its monotonous call from a treetop; wrens flickered squeaking over the tops of stone walls; a grey wagtail bobbed and wagged on the towpath ahead of us; *tee-tee-tee* high overhead alerted us to the passage of a flock of long-tailed tits; and we saw quite a few oddly silent blackbirds.

A golf course came into sight on the left, and the canal ran into a cutting lined by high buttressed walls clothed with old ivy grown into dark green towers and spires. Ahead was Foden Bank Bridge, looking quite ordinary from this side, but on passing through we found it was a superb roving bridge: the stone walls and cobbled path climbing, crossing, curling and looping back under themselves. Just by the bridge was a weatherbeaten milestone measuring 12 miles from Marple and we couldn't quite read how many to Hall Green.

The roving bridges, also known as change line bridges, turnover bridges, or snake bridges, were designed to take the towpath from one side of the canal to the other in such a way as to make it unnecessary to unhitch the horse. Leisurely as the old canal transport may seem to our 21st century eyes, saving time was actually a prime consideration for the working boat-man. The turnover bridge is not quite unique to the Macclesfield canal; but the simple grace of the Macclesfield's six examples puts them in a class of their own. Their beauty of line is often ascribed to Thomas Telford (right), the design engineer for the canal, but more credit, according to Hadfield, should go to William Crossley, the supervising engineer when the canal was actually built.[1] The latter was responsible for the detail and finish; Telford dealt more with the initial and general survey and plan. He had to deal with the landowners through whose property the canal would run, and found the Cheshire gentry to be of 'an unaccommodating disposition…in persisting to prohibit the proper line of the canal'.[2]

The Macclesfield was a very late canal, three previous schemes having been scuppered by vested interests (in particular the Trent & Mersey Canal) opposing the plans in Parliament. The fourth, successful, attempt led to the canal being built in the late 1820s, by which time all kinds of lessons (such as this very long summit level) had been learned during the construction and subsequent operation of earlier canals.

24th December 2002

We returned to the milestone four days later to continue the walk, having left the turkey taking its time in the oven. It was a fair-sized bird, since we'd somehow managed to invite sixteen (mostly Chinese) students to Christmas morning service followed by traditional British Christmas dinner. Ishbel didn't really fancy cooking for Christmas Eve as well, so the idea was to head out for a walk and lunch while the weather was nice and sunny. By the time we got walking it wasn't sunny any more, of course, but at least it was mild and breezy – good walking weather.

Or good training run weather: a tall young woman came striding past us in a tracksuit; you couldn't call that jogging, it was a good strong ground-covering stride. We saw her returning half an hour later, rather more mud-spattered, but no more out of breath: impressive, and we might only have seen a fraction of the session. Ishbel wanted to know if she'd looked as impressive as that when we lived in Sweden and she was training for the local half-marathon. Of course she had.

Round the corner from Foden Bank Bridge was Gurnett aqueduct, which spanned the River Bollin, and was rebuilt a few years ago, providing good moorings for passing boats. Tied up were *Liberty* of Great Haywood; *Serendipity; Lolipop* (sic); *Rosie;* and *August Rose*; and two aged anglers sat with stoical immobility and infinite patience, staring at the brown water.

[1] Hadfield, C (1966) *The Canals of the West Midlands* David & Charles
[2] Cheshire County Council (1986) *Rail, Water & Tramways*

The Macclesfield Canal Guide alerted us to a historic building on the road under the aqueduct: Plough House, visible from the towpath when you know which one it is. It identified itself with a stone plaque bearing the legend:

ON THESE PREMISES
1733 – 1740
JAMES BRINDLEY
THE FAMOUS CIVIL ENGINEER
AND CANAL BUILDER SERVED
AS APPRENTICE TO ABRAHAM
BENNETT

At the time, Brindley was learning the millwright's craft; canal building was still some way in the future. But it was an appropriate grounding: the millwright had to be able to master iron, wood and water, earth and stone; all the materials and principles underlying the canal engineer's problem-solving expertise. From an early stage in his apprenticeship, Brindley was already showing his desire to make structures that would last, to the despair of his master, who preferred to rely on the prospect of future work repairing what had been first attempted. 'Jem,' he admonished young Brindley, 'if thou persist in this foolish way of working, there'll be very little trade left to be done when thou comes out of thy time. Thou knows that firmness of wark's the ruin o' trade!'[1]

Around Plough House clustered the village of Sutton; this is where Elisabeth Gardner, my great-great-great-great-great-great-great-great-grandmother mentioned in the last chapter, lived before she was married three hundred and fifty years ago.

Another historic building tucked almost directly under the aqueduct was the Old King's Head, proudly proclaiming itself 'a Coaching House and Smithy from 1695'. It was no longer a smithy, of course, but we could see the stone arch (glassed in now) where the forge would have been.

It certainly still provided good fare for travellers, prompting a switch into restaurant-review mode: *my companion chose the roast lamb with mint sauce and gravy, sprouts, carrots and new potatoes, while I opted for the tagliatelle in tomato, mushroom and parsley sauce accompanied by herb bread. Everything was freshly cooked, piping hot, and very tasty; and I decided to follow with mulled wine cheesecake, while my companion, after due consideration, plumped for the brandy snap basket with fruit salad and champagne sorbet. A spoonful of each other's dessert helped convince us that both were delicious; and the final bill, at just over £20 including drinks, was very reasonable indeed for food of this standard.*

I was forced to admit that the cheesecake was not quite as good as Ishbel's home-made; but it was very good all the same. And the Banks's was *excellent*: how do they get so much flavour into a half-pint glass?

According to one website, 'many real ale buffs turn their noses up at Banks's beer but it is possible to get excellent pints when the cellarwork is done properly.'

---

[1] Bode, H (2ed 1980) *James Brindley* Shire

For myself, the taste brings back memories of another of Chris Parker's barge trips through Wolverhampton in 1979, when Banks's and Hanson's were still separately brewed, although in the same company, and you could taste the difference and try and decide which you preferred. I never could make my mind up. 'To the dismay of many', says the website, Banks finally closed Hanson's brewery in 1991.

So now I never will know which I prefer; still, Banks's is satisfying, and the website saved the exertion of trying to describe a taste: 'a good balance... its hoppiness and the slight bittersweet aftertaste'. I was going to say that something about it put me in mind of the smell of fresh straw, but that doesn't really do it justice. A last nugget of information from the website: this 3.8% bitter is 'aimed at 26-45 year-old men who drink out often'. If they hit me, that doesn't say much for their aim. Memo: challenge Banks's marketing department to a game of arrows sometime.

Beyond the aqueduct was another beautiful stone bridge (No 44, Leek Old Road Bridge), which on closer inspection was not only a fine outline but brilliant engineering as well: the bridge was on a skew, and standing underneath we could see the curves of the rising courses, built at just the right angle to keep the perfect oval profile slantways under the road. As so often, the solution of an engineering problem gave great beauty of line, which was further enhanced by the beauty of the grey stone building blocks.

On the other side of the bridge was *Ivy*, an old narrowboat which looked as if it had been converted from a working wooden motor. The canal stretched ahead across an open plain of green meadows liberally sprinkled with rooks and sheep. Gaggles of Canada geese swept this way and that under high grey clouds, honking to each other and finally congregating noisily, over a hundred strong, in the lowest part of the meadow. The wind bent the stems of the rushes at the canal's edge, and blew the straw-coloured leaves stiffly sideways. In one direction we could see the stands and floodlights of Macclesfield Town's ground; in the other the hills rose, clothed in sombre greens and browns, up to Tegg's Nose.

Two little old ladies passed us, accompanied by three little old dogs, one of which had a strap round its muzzle; we wondered whether it had a tendency to bite people, or to scavenge food it shouldn't, or maybe just to pull harder than appropriate with a little old lady on the other end of the lead. Near Leek New Road Bridge (another superb skew design) were a few houses with canal frontages; some gardens that would be gorgeous in the summer, and were still worth a look even in December, including a weeping willow and a group of silver birches. Less picturesque was the old white van at the top of the bank, which had obviously been there for some years. It was gaining a dull green-brown patina, but was not yet fully absorbed by the surrounding plant life.

4th January 2003

We returned to the same bridge at Lyme Green in much more wintry weather: a thin covering of snow everywhere and the temperature somewhere around zero. In the circumstances the nearby Silkmen did very well to get their 3rd round FA Cup tie against Watford under way – though perhaps in the end they wished they hadn't, for Watford won 2-0.

But as we set off that was still a few hours in the future; it was late morning, crisp and bright, and no doubt the local footballers and supporters were still dreaming of giant-killing exploits (yes, from Macclesfield's perspective Watford counted as a giant; a nice manageable little giant, they probably thought). Meanwhile we glanced up at the snow-covered hills, down at the snow-covered canal, and set off along the towpath. Other walkers passed and greeted us, wrapped up well and enjoying this sharp sunny morning. In the field across the canal, a megagaggle of Canada geese stirred restlessly, then with one accord took off and whirred overhead, dropping a cluster of guano bomblets over the canal. We were glad to have been missed.

A blackbird posed in the bare hawthorn hedge, showing off inky black plumage and a bright orange bill. He took a scarlet haw in his beak, froze for a moment, then gulped it down. The stark colours recalled Bottom's description in *A Midsummer Night's Dream*: 'The ousel-cock, so black of hue, with orange-tawny bill'. As we approached Broadhurst the canal came close to the former North Staffordshire railway, now electrified. The sound of an outboard motor heralded a small white cruiser: *Mermaid*, breaking a dark path through the thin white skin of ice.

Broadhurst Swing Bridge was the last remaining of the Macclesfield Canal's many swing bridges, and had been restored by the Canal Society in the 1990s. It looked very smart, with a little black plaque saying BWB 1998 NORTHWICH, and was picturesquely framed by bare trees that allowed a clear view of an interesting house beyond. We turned away and climbed a stile to a path, which took us towards a footbridge over the railway. It looked as if the path might be soggy underfoot, but the frost was just hard enough for us to tiptoe across the crust of snow and ice without breaking through to the black morass below.

A Virgin train droned by, accelerating. Seventy years ago, say, at that time of day, it might have been the one named express of the day that went from Manchester to London via Stoke: 'The Lancastrian', perhaps hauled by a brand new 'Jubilee' in shining crimson lake livery, triple-time exhaust echoing across the plain: 'a most exhilarating ferocious tearing roar' is Essery's description of the sound of a Jubilee being pushed hard by her driver.[1] The Jubilees were among Stanier's first designs, and with their Swindon-inspired taper boilers looked unlike anything the London, Midland & Scottish had seen before. They had some teething problems with poor steaming, but once these were sorted out they were fast and powerful performers, whose only weakness was a tendency of the inside big end to overheat. The ingenious and odoriferous answer to this problem was garlic stuffed in a hole in the crank pin, which would in theory release a stink bomb effect when the metal became really hot.

Ninety years ago there was already a Manchester-Euston express that went via Stoke under an agreement between the LNWR and the North Staffordshire Railway.

[1] Essery, T (1996) *Steam Locomotives Compared* Atlantic

The NSR provided the motive power for the first part of the southward journey, as a photo published in Rex Christiansen's *Portrait of the North Staffordshire Railway* proves. It's black and white, of course, so you have to imagine the deep purple-black, with white upper panels, of the LNWR coaches, and the madder lake NSR livery of the 'H' class 0-6-0, brasswork gleaming as it stormed along. On most railways 0-6-0 locomotives were confined to slow freight and perhaps local passenger trains; but the North Staffordshire seemed to have no embarrassment about polishing them up and asking them to pull expresses: they were certainly strong enough, and by all accounts they had quite a reasonable turn of speed.

Echoes of trains real and imagined died away and we came to the footbridge: a modern affair in plain sheet steel, painted an unobtrusive shade of green; presumably it had been put in when the line was electrified. Even the graffiti were environmentally considerate, being confined to the inside of the walkway. On the sensible non-slip floor shiny letters proclaimed that Grant ♥ Teresa. We saw no evidence to reassure us about Teresa's reciprocal feelings; perhaps she didn't get a turn with the paint can till it was empty.

From the top of the footbridge were fine views of the snow-blanketed and mast-topped Croker Hill; and in the opposite direction, a clear view of a landfill site, less than beautiful, but popular with gulls and rooks. On the far side of the bridge we spotted a Stop, Look and Listen sign to indicate what kind of crossing had predated the bridge. Another stile took us into Danes Moss: initially into a bare woodland of low trees, open enough for the snow to have drifted down through the thin branches and carpeted the ground, so that dark twisty trunks stood out against the white. Something about the scene brought the word *tulgy* to mind, but it was hard to say exactly what…

> And as he stood in uffish thought
> The Jabberwock, with eyes of flame
> Came whiffling through the tulgy wood
> And burbled as it came.

Of course, it's all different now. Vorpal blades are illegal – you wouldn't even get away with hemivorpal – and just supposing you had one (under special licence) you still wouldn't be allowed to touch a jabberwock, which would certainly be listed and protected if it wasn't extinct in England (thanks to a beamish boy with no notion of wildlife conservation). Plans for a controlled reintroduction of jabberwocks are probably bogged down in initial discussions over suitable habitat.

Still discussing whether the wood actually was tulgy or not, Ishbel and I found ourselves walking on rotting railway sleepers; and at one point, some lightweight narrow-gauge track was still attached. A large circular plate of rusty metal leant against a birch tree. It was probably what remained of a small (one wagon sized)

37

turntable, and the track would be from the days of peat-cutting. The light track could have been moved about to wherever the cutters were currently working. We were walking along a kind of causeway: the turntable would have been shifted up and down, with tracks running out at right-angles into the Moss. According to Suleman *(op cit)*, peat had been produced here until 1965, which explained why trackwork was still in evidence.

Patches of open water on one side showed where most peat had disappeared; elsewhere reeds and rushes shone bright and sandy in the winter sun. Eventually, as we left the Moss, climbing slightly into pastureland, we passed a notice board explaining how the Cheshire Wildlife Trust had been working to save Danes Moss from the encroachment of the landfill site and the depredations of the peat-cutting. The water table in at least part of the Moss had been restored to a level where characteristic wildlife (all beautifully illustrated on the board) could thrive.

Ahead, the path ran between two tree-lined banks. Round the base of one of the trees popped a fearless little wren, allowing us close enough to see the delicate barred pattern to its plumage. Further on, we found that the frost hadn't affected some of the muddiest bits between the banks, and a deep soft treacly mass stretched right across the track. We were reduced to scrambling halfway up the bank, when we met a King Charles spaniel with a man (who tried the other bank) and a child in wellies, who just ploutered through. As we were nearing the end of the traverse, the spaniel came running back just to check that we were OK. What a thoughtful dog.

Coming to a crosspaths with a similar track between banks, we turned left under denser hollies and oaks. Great tits squeaked above us, and at one point something shot overhead on curved wings – sparrowhawk? We didn't see enough of it to say. Before long we were approaching a road, meeting three Dalmatians in varying shades of spot: dark brown, light brown, and very pale indeed. They had obviously just been let out of a car, and were bouncing around excitedly cocking legs in all directions.

A couple of hundred yards along the road – spotting a blue tit in the hedge on the way – brought us to the beginning of the next footpath, signposted to Gawsworth. It was really time to turn back, but the air was so crisp, and the light such a fine pale gold, that we felt we should make the most of it. Lunch was postponed *sine hora*, and we set off over open pastureland, passing at intervals through galvanised metal gates, thus giving me a little refresher course on the correct and gentlemanly way to proceed through a kissing gate.

In the distance the tower of Gawsworth church was visible through trees. A smell of silage wafted down the breeze to us, and we saw a tractor driving around spreading. A family with an Airedale passed by: this seemed to be dogwalking country. Solitary oak trees stood, each on a tangle of writhen roots, as if the level of the ground around them had fallen by a couple of feet. The last field before Gawsworth had some quite boggy areas, but by keeping close to the hedge, where the ground was still frozen, we stayed dryshod. As we neared the stile by the gate, the tractor came through. 'You doing alright?' the driver asked us.

'Fine, thanks' we answered. 'Lovely day'.
'Grand' he said. 'Smashing.'

A moorhen scuttered across the road and into the pond. Beyond the water the red brick of the New Hall stood imposingly. We decided that we had come far enough, given that we had to retrace our steps and then go and find something to eat.

Gawsworth church

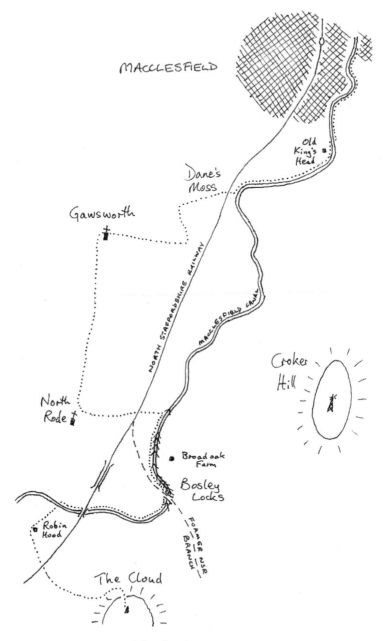

MACCLESFIELD

Old King's Head

Dane's Moss

Gawsworth

NORTH STAFFORDSHIRE RAILWAY

MACCLESFIELD CANAL

Croker Hill

North Rode

Broadoak Farm

Bosley Locks

Robin Hood

FOAMER NSR BRANCH

The Cloud

Map for chapters 3 - 5

Four: Gawsworth to Bosley *(4 miles)*

Lord Flame – The Bishop of Chester's Jig – the ice-tester – Dark Lady – iconoclasm or vandalism – Circumference Hornpipe – distant cloud – lank-eared phantoms – Jack & Jone – snowfall – nutjobber

5th January 2003

The fine weather continued the next day; so although we didn't have too much daylight left after church and lunch, we postponed pudding and washing-up, and came back to the same spot to continue the walk through and beyond Gawsworth. Where we had seen the moorhen the day before, today a Land-Rover piled with logs drove by, with an Alsatian trotting impatiently alongside, clearly finding the vehicle a bit slow.

A little further on, tucked in a corner against a high yew hedge, was a heavy lead ten-foot cast metal statue, and a stone slab nearby, chiselled PEEL. The statue looked as if it had been put there temporarily while a better place was found; we wondered where it had been rescued from.

The road curved round towards New Hall, where 'Maggotty' Johnson once lived, one of the characters of his age, and a true English eccentric. He was one of the very last of the court jesters, a fine dancer and an excellent fiddler. The nickname 'Maggotty' is said to refer to his pock-marked face; but there may also have been a hint at the tunes he liked to play: many tunes at this time were known as Maggots. A Maggot was also a quirky idea, and he had plenty of those. One suggested derivation is the Italian word *magioletta*, a little toy or trifle.

One of Maggotty's patrons was the Bishop of Chester, who presented him with a pound of tea every year. It was valuable stuff at that time, but the Bishop also used to hide ten guineas amongst the tea-leaves, for Johnson's practical support, and perhaps the fiddler played the well-known Bishop of Chester's Jig by way of thanks.

Bishop of Chester's Jig

This kindly music-loving Bishop of Chester was named Samuel Peploe; his arms are given as *Azure, on a chevron counter-embattled between three stringed bugle-horns Or a mitre with labels of the First.* The bugle is a recurrent motif in Cheshire heraldry, perhaps because in medieval times the area included much good hunting territory.

41

Maggotty Johnson wrote a comic opera, *Hurlothrumbo*, which was successful and popular, running for fifty nights in 1729 at the Haymarket in London. As a result he became well-known, and was later called 'Little Samuel Johnson' to distinguish him from the famous Doctor, who was alive at the same period, though somewhat younger. Many came from the south to visit Maggotty in Gawsworth, which helped give him an unquenchable sense of his own importance. He had played the lead role of Lord Flame in *Hurlothrumbo*, and continued to use this name so consistently that some innocent folk imagined him to be a real lord. In later life, his drunkenness and vanity led to very strange and reclusive behaviour.

The plot of land where Maggotty Johnson lies buried was originally intended for his faithful servant/housekeeper; but her brother prevented this. He then wished to be buried there himself, but his wish was not at first respected. A little while after his first burial in consecrated ground he was reinterred where he had wished, at the highest point of a little strip of woodland today owned by the National Trust. It is a pleasant spot, open under tall pines and beech-trees, with hollies dotted here and there, and numerous squirrels who look like red/grey crosses.

A big stone slab rests on a brick plinth. The inscription is a little blurred, but readable:

> Under this stone
>
> Rest the remains of Mr. Samuel Johnson
> Afterwards ennobled by the grander title of
>
> LORD FLAME
>
> Who after being in this life distinct from other men by the
> Eccentricities of his genius
> Chose to retain the same character after his death
> And was, at his own desire, buried here, May 5
> A.D. MDCCLXXXIII - Aged 82
>
> Stay, thou who chance or ease persuades
> To seek the quiet of these sylvan shades
> Here, undisturbed and hid from vulgar eyes,
> A wit, musician, poet, player lies
> A dance-master, alone in grace he shone
> And all the acts of opera were his own.
> In comedy well-skilled, he drew Lord Flame
>
> Acted the part, and gained himself the name
> Averse to strife, how oft he'd gravely say,
> These peaceful groves should shade his breathless clay;
> That when he rose again, here laid alone,
> No friend and he should quarrel for a bone
> Thinking that there were some lame old gossip nigh,
> She possibly might take his leg or thigh.

We didn't, however, visit Maggotty's Wood on this occasion, nor did we visit Gawsworth Hall, though we had been there on other occasions. This fine Tudor timber building has too much of interest to list here, too much to take in at one visit. The overall impression is of the strength and mellow beauty of old wood, some roughly formed and structural, some richly carved. The present owners host many events: craft or antique fairs, classic car rallies, open air music and theatre performances; so there are various opportunities to visit Gawsworth Hall. One unusual memory I have is of taking tea in a small marquee at a craft fair, and seeing that a dragonfly had got in and couldn't quite find a way out. It finally took a rest on the canvas at eye level near the entrance, and I was able to study the green and blue rings of a Southern Hawker from only a few inches' distance.

Gawsworth still has the same dignity that Leo Grindon appreciated well over a century ago: 'the ancient trees, the venerable church, the dignified old residencies, all speak at once of a long-standing and undisturbed respectability such as few villages can now assert'[1]. Approaching the church, we saw a perfect Christmas-card picture on this frosty afternoon: a robin posing in the thorn hedge; snow on the pond and on the wooden fence beyond; snow on the roof of the lych-gate, and the typically English church tower rising over all. Jackdaws flew up to the tower, with their 'chack chack' cries providing the soundtrack to go with the visual effect.

A hair-raising story is told of this pond in the nineteenth century, in similar weather; the pond was frozen, but the young parson was not sure if the ice would bear skating on:

> He called the biggest boy on the bank to go upon the ice; the boy hesitated, but he was urged to go further and further, and then he ordered the boy to jump and jump; the boy was in mortal fear, but he durst not disobey, and at length he jumped again and again till Mr Brandt was satisfied of its strength. He then went into the Rectory and forthwith came back, and putting on his skates he disported himself all afternoon.[2]

Gawsworth church is full of interesting details: one of the most well-known is the tomb of the Fittons that includes among its kneeling effigies Mary Fitton (right), claimed by many (and denied by others) to be the 'Dark Lady' of Shakespeare's sonnets. She was a lady-in-waiting to Elizabeth I, and seems to have had many admirers, whom she encouraged just enough to keep them interested. Eventually she encouraged the Earl of Pembroke a little too much: a contemporary letter comments:

> We have no news but that there is a misfortune befallen Mistress Fitton, for she is proved with child, and the Earl of Pembroke being examined confesseth a fact but utterly renounceth all marriage. I fear they will both dwell in the Tower awhile, for the Queen hath vowed to send them thither.[3]

[1] Grindon, *op cit*
[2] Richards, R (1957) *The Manor of Gawsworth* Ancient Monuments Society
[3] Sir Robert Cecil writing to Sir George Carew

The Earl, William Herbert by name, was one of several Williams chasing the alluring Mary; Sir William Knollys was another; and perhaps Will Shakespeare, which would explain the lines in one of his sonnets:

> Whoever hath her wish, thou hast thy 'Will'
> And 'Will' to boot, and 'Will' in overplus.

On the other hand, there was also William Polwhele, who she eventually married, so there might have been three Wills even without Shakespeare, and he might have written the sonnet for Herbert (who might have been his patron) to present to Mary. The known details are enough to give the story substance, and the unknown enough to make it intriguing; and the controversy will certainly continue.

Mary Fitton was from an old-established family: by marrying a twice-widowed heiress in 1317, Edward Fitton had inherited Gawsworth manor from the de Orreby family, who held it from 1130. The Fittons hung on to the manor until 1663, when the Gerards, Earls of Macclesfield, took over. Among the many coats of arms to be seen in the church are the ancient arms of de Orreby, simple and practical for the battlefield: *Argent, two chevrons and a canton Gules.* The Fitton arms hint at the connection by retaining the canton, though firmly overlaid by a bend dexter, thus breaking the rules of heraldry by putting colour on colour: *Argent, a canton Gules, over all a bend Azure charged with three garbs Or.*

Looking around this fascinating church, interest was sharpened by knowing that in the sixteenth, seventeenth and eighteenth centuries, ancestors of my great-great-great-great-grandfather William Braddock were married here (see the tree on p.56); and presumably also worshipped here, though that is not recorded. The various families (Braddock, Knight, Shaw, Arrowsmith, Baylie, and Passe) did not all live in Gawsworth village: the parish was large, and included several outlying villages, some of which I would soon come to on my route.

In the eighteenth century, and into the early nineteenth, the congregational singing would have been supported by an orchestra, rather than the modern organ; a curate's wife is recorded as commenting on the west gallery's complement of 'every description of musical instrument under the sun'. From churchwardens' accounts these are known to have included flute, clarinet, fiddle and bass viol, but there must have been more than that to provoke comment.

Around the same period, the minister-schoolmaster is described as an enthusiast for music outside the church as well as in; no doubt the same musicians played the same instruments for all occasions, sacred and secular. The Reverend James Crabtree

> …had short legs and a short body, and was very corpulent. I do not doubt that his circumference was far greater than his length. He had a good school, and was reckoned a jovial fellow, and was pretty well liked in the parish. He was frequently invited to the farm houses on their special occasions, such as what they called 'Shutting of Shearing' or Harvest Home. Notwithstanding his great corpulence, he prided himself in knowing how to step it. It was rare fun for the swains,

when all hearts were merry, to see their parson with his big stomach and short legs, and without coat or waistcoat, leading off in an Irish jig, or dancing a hornpipe with the servant-maids.[1]

What music might he have been dancing to? The tune given below came from the notebook of a West Midland fiddler, where it had no name; it might well have been current locally, and we could call it the Circumference Hornpipe in the corpulent curate's honour. Perhaps some of the Braddock family were present as spectators, dancers, or even musicians.

The Circumference Hornpipe

There may be much of interest in the church, but there would have been much more, particularly wall paintings and medieval stained glass, if it had been more carefully conserved. At one time it was thought that the Puritans had indulged in iconoclasm during the Commonwealth period; but more careful research showed that most of the ancient art survived – if somewhat dilapidated – into the nineteenth century, and then disappeared in 1851 as a result of a restoration programme carried out by a zealous but philistine curate and an absentee architect. The architect, Sir Gilbert Scott, had so many commissions under way that he delegated almost everything. Travelling by train, he once spotted a church swathed in scaffolding. Asking his secretary who was working on that church, he received the answer 'You are, Sir.'

A couple more bends in the lane, beyond the church and the pond, and we came to a row of parked cars as well as several mature ramblers sitting on the kerb changing out of their serious boots into ordinary footwear. They were finishing just as we were getting going; but we pressed on undeterred. An old green iron sign was lettered 'Peak District and Northern Counties Footpaths Preservation Society No 149   1964 Footpath to North Rode'. We felt honoured to be following a route kept open by so ancient a pressure group.

---

[1] Richards, *op cit*

A solidly-built ladder stile took us over the bank and into a two-tone field: green where the sun had been on it, white in the shadowed areas. Our route lay across the white, which made for crisp walking. Looking back, Gawsworth church tower glowed in the late sunshine. At the next ladder stile, a small figure descended slowly: fair hair and blue eyes peeped at us suspiciously from under a lumberjack's cap with earmuffs. Wellies and fleecy layers over a camouflage jacket completed the thermal defences. His family urged him on from behind; eventually they were all over the stile and we could take our turn.

The next hour or so provided a lot of practice in how a gentleman helps his companion over different kinds of stiles, both substantial and dilapidated. Gentleman Lessons were arranged for me many years ago by Swiss students at the language school where Ishbel and I worked, when they heard that we were to be married. Sadly, I never completed the course. There seemed to be an awful lot of modules; maybe when I retire…?

The smoky grey outline of The Cloud hung in the distance, too indistinct to be sure if it was snow-covered or not. On a day like this you see why the hill got its name. Coming to a very prickly stile, tucked in a corner and hidden by a dense holly hedge, we looked down on a couple of ponds, fringed by aspen and willow and the red stems of dogwood. The path led past the ponds, up and over a slight rise; The Cloud still ahead, becoming slightly more distinct and less insubstantial as we drew nearer.

Eventually we came to little patches of woodland and three stiles in quick succession near Shellow. Trees and bushes were rooted in deep overgrown stagnant pools, the surface of the water lurid green. Perhaps it was because the light was fading, and the setting sun was hidden behind a low hill, but the place seemed a little depressing; I was reminded of the line from Keats' *Hyperion*:

Oh lank-eared phantoms of black-weeded pools!

Not that we saw any phantoms, but if we had, they would have been lank-eared. We turned back, and walked back up into the light of the sun, as it went down on our left in rosy splendour.

8th January 2003

I returned alone to the stile near Shellow three days later: the weather no warmer; colder if anything, with a dusting of fresh snow on the ground, and in fact it was snowing as I set off, a light, dry, powdery snow that soon died away. Two rabbits scampered into a clearing beyond the stile, then bolted in opposite directions.

As I came to the next stile, a wren perched on barbed wire very close by, tail cocked; then dived into a crack in the bark of an oak. It seems to be natural to feel warm and protective towards the jaunty little wren – so tiny, so vulnerable, so energetic and enthusiastic. Jenny Wren, it is often called; Kitty Wren, Bewick called it; *motacilla troglodytes*, Linnaeus called it, more dispassionately.

The ground was frozen hard and nubbly to walk on; ice stood in ruts and puddles; a bare oak leaned over a small frozen pool. Soon I came to Rode Green, and walked a few yards along Pexall Road, past a couple of handsome brick houses, before finding a clear signpost to North Rode, and another stile. Despite the cold, there was abundant birdlife all through this morning's walk: great tits, robins, sparrows, blackbirds, pigeons, rooks, crows, fieldfare and redwing.

The country was open and I had clear views of Croker Hill, away to my left, and The Cloud, more or less straight ahead, becoming clearer as the distance lessened.

After Manor Farm I found myself on a concrete track – no harder than the fields alongside, on a day like this – and then the tower of North Rode church, with its distinctive turret on one side, appeared in silhouette behind a group of pines. Somewhere around here – for they are listed in Gawsworth parish register as 'of Rode' – lived the earliest ancestors of William Braddock I have yet found. John Passe married Joane Lowndes in 1559, so they must both have been born in the reign of Henry VIII. They had nine children, of whom at least four died young. The couple's names recall Thomas Campian's charming song, though the children's names are different. The Passes' everyday country life is unlikely to have been as idyllic as the song suggests, though there is no reason to suppose they were unhappy, nor that they were ever as hungry and desperate as their descendents the Linneys, nearly three hundred years later in industrial Denton (see Book 2, chapter 8).

Jack and Jone

Thomas Campian, 1613

Jack and Jone they think no ill,
But loving live and merry still;
Do their week days work and pray
Devoutly on the holy day:
Skip and trip it on the green,
And help to choose the Summer Queene;
Lash out at a country feaste
Their silver penny with the best.

Jone can call by name her cowes,
And deck her windowes with green boughs,
Shee can wreathes and tuttyes make
And trimme with plums a Bridall cake.
Jack knows what brings gain or loss
And his long Flaile can stoutly tosse
Make the hedge which others breake
And ever thinkes what he doth speake.

Well can they judge of nappy ale,
And tell at large a Winter tale,
Climb up to the apple loft
And turn the crabs till they be soft.
Tib is all the farmer's joy
And little Tom the mother's boy
All their pleasure is content
And care to pay their yearely rent

Now you worthy Dames and Knights
That study only strange delights,
Though you scorn the home-spun gray
And revell in your rich array
Though your tongues dissemble deepe
And can your heads from danger keepe
Yet for all your pompe and traine
Securer lives the silly Swaine.

My route was about to bend sharply left before North Rode, and I saw from the map that I could cut the corner, heading straight for the trees down to my left. As I veered across the field, it began to snow quite thickly (not heavily, the flakes were big but light and dry, brushing off easily), reducing visibility so that I was relieved to spot the path I had cut the corner to. This led into the driveway from Manor House, which took me past plantations and an ornamental lake, frozen over and pure white in the freshly falling snow, through a gateway with big urn-topped gateposts, out to the road. The snow stopped, and was quickly succeeded by sunshine.

At this point the road crossed the railway, by the site of what had once been North Rode station. The exceptionally tall station building, which once towered over the road though it stood at rail level below, had long since been demolished, and there was little trace of it. This had been the junction station for the Churnet Valley line of the North Staffordshire, and when that was closed in the early sixties, North Rode station was redundant.

Beyond the railway, to the left of the road, was a long plantation, marked on an old map with the wonderfully ambiguous name of Big Dog Bottom Wood (which is big, the wood or the dog, or…?). The wood was well filled with rhododendron and holly under the taller trees. A robin, fluffed out so that he was completely spherical, popped out onto the verge of the road and glared belligerently. On a branch above, a nuthatch showed off its colours in the sun, the lines of eye-stripe and bill giving it that characteristic streamlined look. Bewick says that it's also known as 'woodcracker', or 'nutjobber', and adds details of all the colours:

The length is near six inches; bill strong, black above, beneath almost white; the eyes hazel; a black stroke passes over each eye, from the bill, extending down the side of the neck as far as the shoulder; all the upper part of the body is of a fine blue grey; the cheeks and chin white; breast and belly of a pale orange; sides marked with streaks of chestnut; quills dusky; the tail is short, the two middle feathers grey, the rest dusky, three of the outermost spotted with white; legs pale yellow; claws large, sharp, and much bent, the back claw very strong…[1]

Very soon I was at the Macclesfield Canal again, by Bosley Top Lock. Moored nearby were *Noah, The Tippler, Wanderer, Parys,* and *Tilly 2.* A BWB sign announced that these were long-term moorings; they certainly looked it: alongside *Parys* the towpath verges had been turned into miniature gardens. I turned and walked down the flight. The long pound between the top lock and No 2 was frozen and snow-covered, but you could just see where a boat had broken a path through, which had then refrozen. The sunshine was pleasant, and the locks photogenic: beautifully designed by Crossley, with double top gates, so that the flight would be worked by a lock-keeper on one side, and the boatman on the other. These twelve locks lift the canal a total of 118 feet, and were grouped together to allow the longest possible summit level (sixteen miles), which was (and is) important for water conservation.

I soon found myself at Lock 5, by Peckerpool Wood Bridge, where Ishbel and I had begun a walk in fine summer weather, more than four months before.

---

[1] Bewick, T (1826) *A History of British Birds*

Five: Bosley Locks to The Cloud *(3½ miles)*

Narrowboat nomenclature – foiling Hitler – the distinctiveness of warblers – hazards of migration – Marston's union system – Glaswegian umbellifer theory – steepness – primitive Methodism – Navvy on the Line – Braddocks from Broadoak? – leisure majestic and infinite – farewell to Cheshire

26th August 2002

I walked from Bosley locks to The Cloud together with Ishbel one August Bank Holiday Monday. We parked up near Peckerpool Wood Bridge and headed down, watching the boats as we strolled past lock after lock. There were so many boats moving that we didn't admire Crossley's engineering as much as we might have done. The locks were grouped together in a single flight of twelve so that the summit level could be as long as possible; and they were constructed for durability and smoothness of operation, using huge stone blocks quarried from The Cloud. What we noticed more was how green the surroundings were, locks and pounds enclosed by lush turf, reeds and rushes, and hawthorn hedges. We also saw orange balsam, *impatiens capensis,* and something else growing in the water by a weir that we thought might have been gipsywort, *lycopus europaeus* – a member of the mint family that appears to have no special uses. It had clusters of little white flowers close to longish stems with many leaves.

I hadn't brought pen or paper, so memorising the names of the boats on the move became quite challenging; luckily I've always loved lists of names. In the lock flight we saw *Josephine, Redwing, Orion, Cindy* and *Moonfleet; Dawdle, Wea-Ry-Tired, William Paterson, Oki Doki, Daisy* and *Filos.* Beyond the bottom lock we passed *Jervaulx, Why Worry, Tasha Lee* and a nameless little day boat from Sherborne Wharf, packed with passengers. I didn't try to memorise all the boats moored between the bottom lock and Old Driving Lane Bridge, but *Serendipity* and *Jubilation* stuck in my mind anyway. Later on, as we came back up the locks, we passed *Fairwater, Stourport, September Morn,* and *Halloween.*

It's embarrassing to admit that at first I considered *Wea-Ry-Tired* to be a rather negative name, and didn't see the groanworthy pun for quite some time. Considering that I grew up in Brixham, where half the houses have names like *Dunroamin* or *Koh-zee-kot* or *Erzanmyne* (genuine examples, those last two, I'm not making them up), this kind of thing ought to stand out immediately. I didn't like to ask who might have been responsible for the pun, but every name might tell a story, and I took the chance to ask about one or two others; though with so many boats on the move people tended to be slightly less open and chatty than when you pass one boat on its own.

I asked the steersman of *Filos*; Greek for 'friend', he said, but I didn't learn any more as the lock gates were open and he was on his way. I also asked one of the crew of *Fairwater*, because I was in Fairwater House at school, and wondered if that had anything to do with it; but no, the boat was borrowed from a friend, who had named it for someone else who had died and who came from a district of Cardiff called Fairwater.

I didn't follow all the story; it was quite a long one. The boat had certainly come a long way, its big scrolled capitals proclaiming 'Caen Hill' below *Fairwater*. A tiny fluffy puppy sat on the roof looking heartmeltingly cute.

Dawdle was obviously very new, gleaming everywhere as if just out of the packing. A couple of months old, said the owner, but with a few scratches on it already. 'Within the first twenty minutes,' put in his other half. Like a new car, he rejoined, you're on tenterhooks till it gets its first bump, so better bump it straightaway. I didn't disagree; it was his boat, and I couldn't see any scratches on it anyway. They must have been so slight that only a new owner would notice.

Most of the boats seemed either new or at least modern purpose-built narrowboats, though the gently rising curve of *William Paterson*, the bows riding higher than the stern, suggested that it might have been converted from a working boat. *Cindy* and *Moonfleet* were smaller cabin cruisers, which were able to fit in the locks together, nose to tail. *Daisy* was for sale, a notice in the window giving very full details of all her measurements and equipment - but no price. I didn't ask in case they thought I was interested. Any narrowboat we could afford would be a total wreck.

The canal turned right under an iron girder bridge that once carried the North Staffordshire Railway's Churnet Valley line; in the next chapter we'll be walking along the trackbed. Beyond the bridge was the bottom lock, where the Macclesfield Canal Society had set up a stall, selling T-shirts, books and brochures and so on, and displaying photos of some of the restoration they'd done. A sterling example was locating, disinterring, and reinstating all the old stone mileposts on the canal, which had been buried as a precaution during the Second World War. We wondered whether the men who had carefully buried them were conscious of the impact on Hitler's plans that their action might have ('Thunderweather! Without the on the Macclesfieldcanal befindly Milestones will our Sabotagetroops themselves hopeless forlose!').

I bought a fascinating historical canal map, and a couple of booklets, and got scolded by Ishbel for not making a bigger donation. The canal ran on along a high straight embankment lined with moored boats; the embankment was taking us over the River Dane, but from the towpath we couldn't see the elegance of the stone aqueduct. Here there had been a serious leak in 1962, just when the future of the Macclesfield Canal hung in the balance because the damage to Marple Aqueduct (and the state of Marple Locks) had rendered the Peak Forest Canal impassable. However the leak here at Bosley was swiftly repaired; Suleman surmises that the anti-canal lobby down south were unaware of the extra excuse to close the canal until it had already been repaired.[1]

---

[1] Suleman, *op cit*

Moving on, we looked up at The Cloud, now looming some seven hundred feet above us, and appearing seriously steep, and wondered if we would come into the category of 'those with the puff to climb those craggy heights', as the Macclesfield Canal Society guide to the canal so encouragingly put it.

The guide also advised us to 'notice the new (1997) footbridge across the spillway just before Old Driving Lane Bridge', so we did that – a fine piece of work – and we also noticed the profusion of water plants filling the spillway, as well as the piping of small birds in the surrounding trees. They were little brown birds with paler chests, making plaintive *oo-ee* sounds: some kind of warbler, I guessed, but I can't tell one from another. Back at home, the bird book explained that the call of the  Willow Warbler (left) is a 'plaintive *fooeed*', while, in stark contrast, the call of the Chiffchaff is a 'plaintive *hooeed*'. How embarrassing not to be able to hear any initial consonant at all. No wonder twitchers twitch, if they have to concentrate hard enough to tell /f/ from /h/ in birdsong. Confusingly, Hugh Falkus says 'The delicate *tuee, tuee* of the willow warbler is very similar to the call of the chiffchaff'[1]. To be fair, the song of the two is rather more different, but I didn't hear any singing, only calling.

I should have heeded the wise dictum of Bill Oddie: 'it's not too difficult to depict in a book what a bird *looks* like... but it's damned near impossible to write down what it *sounds* like!'[2] So perhaps they were Bonelli's Warblers, whose call is a 'rather plaintive *hoo-eet*', even though I didn't hear any /t/ at the end. Bonelli's Warblers are pretty rare in England, so according to Bill Oddie that would be a 'megatick'; but perhaps I would just lay myself open to accusations of 'stringing' – a heinous ornithological crime. Safer to assume they were Willow Warblers, the likeliest option given the habitat.

Willow warblers, says Thorburn[3], migrate to Ethiopian Africa, but not over the equator. So in a few weeks, when the days grew yet shorter, and the sun less warm, these little brown birds would be off, maybe down to Gibraltar and across the Sahara, or maybe via Turkey and Palestine to Egypt, thence to follow the Nile southwards. Would they be startled by gunfire in Gaza? Would they see the smoke from burning villages in the Sudan? Or would they find a route that only took them past places as peaceful as this corner of the Macclesfield Canal?

At least the small birds are not as actively persecuted as they once were. The Honourable John Byng, ahead of his time in his environmental views, expressed scorn in 1790 for those that saw birds only as a nuisance:

> The race of birds will be quickly extinct ... as ignorance is the offspring of barbarity, the farmer and gardener are taught to believe that all birds rob and plunder them, and that they should be destroyed by every engine, and scared away by every invention.

[1] Falkus, H (1980) *Nature Detective* Penguin
[2] Oddie, W (2ed 1995) *Little Black Bird Book* Robson
[3] Fisher, J ed (1967) *Thorburn's Birds* Michael Joseph

By these means the country is stript of a chief beauty; and the contemplative man misses a prime satisfaction. –On the few remaining tall trees the rook is forbid to build! The blackbird and bullfinch are shot in the kitchen garden! The sparrow is limed in the farm yard! And the swallow is driven from 'the coigne of vantage'! Now would these blockheads but consider the works of Providence who sends all things for our uses, or comforts, they might observe … that these birds independent of the pleasure from their song, their flight, and their company, are of several most material uses. –The rook (in my opinion) does one shillingsworth of advantage, by destruction of the slug, for a pennyworth of damage sustained by the corn.[1]

The big question now facing us was whether to leave the towpath at Bridge 57, Old Driving Lane Bridge, climb The Cloud, and have lunch in a pub on the way down; or to continue to Bridge 61, and have lunch before tackling the ascent. Consulting watches and stomachs, we opted for the latter, and headed on along the towpath, pausing only to admire a Peacock butterfly, its maroon , white and black as bright as any new narrowboat, posing on purple knapweed. Further on a heron took off and circled round behind us, reappearing in a meadow beyond the far bank. At Crossley Hall Farm martins were swooping over the canal and around the mellowed redbrick Tudor buildings: a very *red* redbrick you see in this part of the country, not quite poppy red, maybe ripe eating apple red…

I warned Ishbel that we had to walk a little way along a main road from Bridge 61 to the pub: Nicholson's, the regional canal guide, reckoned 10 minutes' walk. 'Is that ten minutes for long legs or ten minutes for little legs?' she wanted to know, but Nicholson's wasn't that explicit. The traffic was fast and unforgiving, and the grass verges very tussocky, but even so, both long and little legs made it to the Robin Hood in seven minutes. Marston's Bitter ('a nice crystal malt character that adds some fullness') and brown bread crispy bacon sandwiches made very acceptable fuel for the forthcoming climb.

After Banks's, Marston's is the second of the Midland beers we have come across, confirming that we have probably crossed a beershed between Northern beerflow and Midland. Marston's causes real ale fanatics to grow particularly lyrical, especially on the internet, where writers can dilate and expand (the quotation below is severely abridged):

> The mere sight of the working unions can move even the most jaded beer hunter to awe and silence. You are in the presence of the last of a species…
>
> For all its apparent quirkiness, the Burton Union system is the natural result of experience and experimentation... Through centuries, brewers had been frustrated as beer and yeast were expelled and lost during active fermentation. One solution was to place buckets or troughs below the barrels, but you still had to manually return the beer to the wood and scoop up the yeast to use in future batches. The union system cleverly sidestepped this limitation. By turning a cask on its side, you could run a swan-necked pipe from the open bung to a trough suspended above.

---

[1] Andrews, *op cit*

If the trough was tilted slightly, liquid could flow back into the cask while the excess yeast would be left behind. Beer and yeast would continue to circulate automatically until fermentation completed. Because so much of the yeast was

eventually left in the trough, the beer in the cask was clearer. In larger-scale production, the basic set-up was expanded to link multiple casks together, 'in union.' At Marston's, the casks are in twin rows of 10-12, each holding 144 Imperial gallons and linked by pipes and long troughs suspended above and below.

What a lot there is to say about Marston's beer; but we had no time to sit and ponder, we had a hill to climb. Turning away from the main road, the noise of traffic quickly died away, and the lanes were quieter than we had feared. We went along Sprink Lane, and then Pedley Lane; passing a little Wesleyan chapel built in 1845, and enjoying the hedge-row flowers: the creamy honeysuckle, purple tufted vetch, and yellow vetchling; the clustered white flowers of hogweed and the flat-topped white umbels of what might have been yarrow; though the sheer number of white umbellifers is very confusing. Ishbel has a theory that all white umbellifers are cow-parsley, a theory that has the virtue of simplicity (William of Ockham would applaud), and one that may not be found wanting in Govanhill, but my flower book disagrees extensively.

The slope increased gradually at first, and then progressively; and the crag at the summit began to rear over us like the crest of a breaking wave. At the junction of Peover Lane and Red Lane was a National Trust sign and a stile, and a path that seemed to be heading straight for the summit. This really was steep, like a straight staircase in a narrow house, and needed a lot of puff and pauses here and there to take in the view at our backs. As we climbed we were in a leafy tunnel of birch and bracken, ling and whortleberry bushes. Further up the birch thinned out but the ling deepened, until eventually we came out at the foot of the topmost crag, where a left turn took us to a gully of tumbled rock which gave access to the summit.

Once up, we realised that the summit area was much bigger than it had looked; and that there were more people up here than we had expected; and that we had obviously come up the hard way: gentler paths led east and south-west. Folk sat on the gritstone slabs in family groups, or strolled around looking at the view of hills to the north and the Cheshire plain to the west. A sizeable model glider wheeled and soared on the upcurrents beyond the crag - presumably radio-controlled? After a few moments we spotted the man with the remote, not far away.

Views extended in all directions: south and west was an equally tall hill over-looking the Cheshire plain. In 1754 Mow Cop was chosen as the site of a fake ruin, the Folly of Squire Wilbraham, who was then able to look up from his residence at Rode Hall and see something more romantic than just a steep hill topped by a rock.

At the beginning of the nineteenth century that hilltop became the scene of the Primitive Methodists' open-air meetings, led by men such as the shy Hugh Bourne and the ex-drinker, ex-gambler, ex-womaniser and ex-fighter William Clowes (right).

The meetings led to many conversions and scenes of great enthusiasm, which shocked the local Methodists to the degree that they soon expelled Bourne and Clowes from the Methodist movement – forgetting that their own churches had been founded only a couple of generations earlier by the open-air-preaching and enthusiasm-generating Wesleys and Whitefield. As a result Primitive Methodism became a separate movement, and instead of this division weakening the church, both Wesleyan and Primitive congregations saw revivals and great growth in this area in the nineteenth century.

North-westwards, in the distance, was the tower of Gawsworth church; and north and east rose the hills, many of them taller than the hill we were standing on. Dominating the view in that direction was the bulk of Croker Hill, topped by its radio mast. Below gleamed the waters of Bosley reservoir, created to supply water to the Macclesfield canal; and by the reservoir was the village of Bosley. In earlier times this was within the parish of Gawsworth; and entries in the parish register make it clear that the Braddocks – a branch of my family tree that we've encountered already – were based in Bosley by the seventeenth century, and probably before that. The interesting point is that one of the farmsteads in Bosley, quite close to Bosley Locks, is called Broadoak, which is the origin of the Braddock surname. Of course there are many farms that go by the name of Broad Oak; there's even another one a few miles further north; but if Braddocks were already in Bosley three or four hundred years ago, it seems plausible that they were there a couple of hundred years earlier still, in the days when surnames were becoming fixed, and that the family took its name from its farm here in Bosley. Another branch of the Braddock family, the Shaws, also came from Bosley; the tree is given overleaf.

To the right of Croker Hill, further away and higher, was the curious flat top of Shuttlingslow, 'that beautiful mamelon', as Leo Grindon *(op cit)* calls it. It is a landmark that can be seen from many points in East Cheshire. This I knew as the scene of the climax of Alan Garner's *Weirdstone of Brisingamen*, a children's fantasy that came out when I was ten, and that delighted me with its dwarfs, goblins, wizards, trolls and witches. I won't give away the story, but after reading it, you would look suspiciously at any crow or scarecrow. Today's generation of Harry Potter fans, if they still haven't had enough after reading all seven books, could do worse than try Garner's first two books, set here in the Cheshire hill country.

Somewhere on the slopes below Shuttlingslow was the village of Wincle, home to the Gardners, another branch of the Braddock tree. So this whole panorama was full of my ancestors: one thick taproot and a lot of rootlets. Bosley, at the time of the Domesday survey, was described as 'waste', and was held by Hugh de Mara.

A generation earlier, in Edward the Confessor's time, the Saxon Godric had held land worth twenty shillings. Did any of my ancestors hold on from Godric's time, through the destruction, to build up their smallholdings again under the Normans? Or was the land effectively cleared, with new men brought in to rebuild? On that question hangs whether the family roots might go back more than a thousand years in this area.

Ancestors of William Braddock

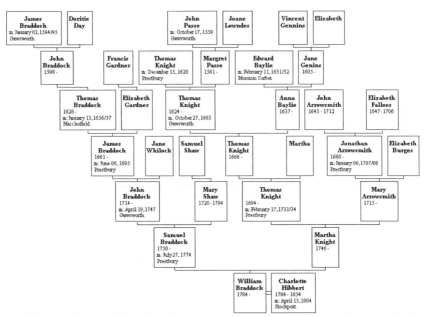

Westwards the Cheshire plain, green and rolling, extended to the limit of visibility; closer below could be seen the line of the canal, with boats moving here and there. The long viaduct beyond the canal was one of the more challenging engineering tasks on the North Staffordshire Railway: twenty arches with a maximum height of 106 feet and a total length of 1,255 feet. The route had been surveyed by the famous George Stephenson, and the contractor was his friend, the almost equally famous Thomas Brassey.

Brassey (left) was the greatest of the railway contractors, who had work in hand everywhere, and at the peak of his career employed tens of thousands of navvies. He not only built one-sixth of the entire rail network in Britain, but worked throughout the world. He fulfilled contracts in France, Italy, Spain, Holland, Prussia and Canada, and made millions (hundreds of millions, in today's money), quite apart from being awarded the Legion of Honour, the cross of the Order of St Maurice and St Lazarus, and the Iron Crown of Austria.

If we had been standing on the Cloud in the late eighteen-forties, we could have seen North Rode Viaduct half-finished, with the navvies swarming like bees around their gigantic task, surely taking extra care and using the best mortar after the collapse of the Barentin viaduct on an earlier contract of Brassey's, the Paris – Le Havre railway.

Thinking of navvying brought back memories of loading freshly-blasted rock by hand into skips as a volunteer on the Festiniog Deviation, as well as a celebratory tune that Ishbel and I sometimes play with friends, a fine hornpipe that combines with the *Kirkgate* (see Book One), or *Kershaw's* and *Taylor's* (see Book Two), or can follow the *Factory Smoke* (see page 117):

Navvy on the Line

It was time to move on. Our route led us eastwards and gently downwards; soon a signpost and little circular plaques told us that we were on both the Gritstone Trail and the Staffordshire Way; and then we headed down a long flight of stone steps. In the lane below we came to the stile where the Gritstone Trail and Staffordshire Way headed off east, while we needed to go north to get back to the car; we could start again at this point another day.

Without realising it, we had entered Staffordshire on beginning the descent from the summit of The Cloud. We should have been more aware of being in such a fine county…

> What a county of modest, unnoticed rivers! What a natural, simple county, content to fix its boundaries by these tortuous island brooks, with their comfortable names - Trent, Mease, Dove, Tern, Dane, Mees, Stour, Tame…
>
> It has everything that England has, including thirty miles of Watling Street; and England can show nothing more beautiful and nothing uglier than the works of nature and the works of man to be seen within the limits of the county.

Thus Arnold Bennett's eulogy in *The Old Wives' Tale*; and as I walked through the county I would be able to see whether it still stood up to such praise. Much had changed since Bennett's day: one would no longer expect to find a 'scattered multitude' of 'thousands of labourers' in the fields; but I would surely see 'long, narrow boats passing in a leisure majestic and infinite over the surface of the stolid canals'. The leisure today may be more real and less apparent.

Six: The Cloud to Rudyard *(5 miles)*

Slipperiness – floty vales – molehillock – not not in the Knot Inn – psychopolitical aspects of spelling – the chemist's daughter's sweetheart's fate – fooling the Duke of Cumberland – swinging on the Gallows Pole – Rudyard Lake – a lady of uncertain age – Steamboat Waltz – the humble bacon butty – when is a wigeon not a wigeon?

9th January 2003

I had leisure to return to the same stile on the flanks of The Cloud some four and a half months later; Ishbel had started back at work a week earlier than me, so I was on my own for a short day's rambling. It was a cold clear winter's day: the view across the valley northwards showed the higher hills with a thin covering of snow, and the lower slopes green; while the north-facing slope I was about to descend bore a dusting of snow almost to the bottom of the valley. Taken all together, a sharp and brightly detailed picture in green and white, picked out in black.

The Gritstone Trail / Staffordshire Way descended quite steeply, with stiles at intervals, and occasional notices reminding walkers that this part of the route is not a public right of way, but private land which the landowner kindly allows Trail and Way to go through. Blessings on the landowner, for this is a wonderful section of footpath where the vista across the valley was constantly in view, but changing in perspective: now set off by large berry-laden hollies; now framed by isolated thorn trees; and the hills opposite growing larger as the path dropped lower.

Sections of boggy ground were spanned by snow-covered duckboards; then there was a short stride across a small morass to a large pointed stepping stone – a step that I would hardly have noticed, much less thought about, in warmer weather. But now the point on which I was to momentarily plant my foot appeared icy, and slipperiness unnerves me. I made it, without disaster, but only after investing rather more determination than two strides ought to warrant.

I met a couple of ramblers, and warned them of the dodgy bit. When they got there they probably wondered what I had been havering about. Meanwhile a snowy grass slope led me down to a lane, where I found that I was now walking *three* trails at once, the Dane Valley Way having joined the other two footpaths. Confusingly (or maybe very cleverly) I was simultaneously heading northwards on the Gritstone Trail; southwards on the Staffordshire Way; and eastwards on the Dane Valley Way.

Round a corner in the lane I came across some curious footprints in the thin layer of snow: like tiny horseshoes open at both ends. I guessed at very small deer; I believe there are both roe deer and muntjak in the area. Consulting Hugh Falkus' *Nature Detective* later didn't help: fine photographs of every kind of footprint except those I'd seen.

The three ways bore right by Raven's Clough and entered the edge of Ravensclough Wood, where the path clung to the edge of a steep slope. Often it only seemed to be dense stands of holly that kept the path in place. Below, the deep valley was filled with birch, oak and ash; birdsong and the sound of tumbling water. It occurred to me to wonder whether 'clough' is actually the same word as 'cleave' (which is what this kind of steep-sided valley is called where I come from, and which is cognate with 'cleft' and 'cliff'). Eventually the path wound down to the valley bottom, crossed the stream on a damp and skiddy wooden bridge where I was glad of a handrail on both sides, and emerged into pastureland alongside a small river: what the Staffordshire Way leaflet evocatively called 'the washland of the Dane'.

Even in this winter season, the surroundings were lovely; the woodland and the meadowland a joy to walk through. A wonderful description in the fourteenth century poem *Pearl* suggests that the poet, who may possibly have been John Massey from Cheshire, took similar delight in country rambling:

> The dubbement dere of doun and dales,
> Of wod and water and wlonk playnes,
> Bylde in me blys, abated my bales,
> Fordidden my stresse, dystryed my paynes.
> Doun after a strem that dryyly hales
> I bowed in blys, bredful my braynes.
> The fyrre I folwed those floty vales,
> The more strengthe of joye myn herte straynes.

(The rich adornment of hill and valleys, of woods and waters and beautiful meadows, built happiness in me and lessened my worries, reduced my stress, destroyed my pains. Down by a stream that flows continually I walked in bliss, my mind brimful. The further I followed those watery valleys, the greater the joy that filled my heart.)

Within the poem, the description is actually part of a dream or vision of heaven: the poet will soon meet the spirit of the dead child he is mourning. But John Massey must have taken great delight in earthly landscape, or he would not have depicted heaven in those terms. Maybe he had once walked or ridden through these same green meadows, over six hundred years ago.

Some way along the Dane valley I noticed a line of molehills, most of them frost-covered, but the end one fresh, which suggested it had been thrown up that morning. As I came up for a closer look, I saw a tiny molehillock a foot or so beyond the fresh one; and focussing more closely, realised that the molehillock was quivering and expanding.

59

I settled down to watch. I've never seen a mole, and although I guessed there wasn't much chance of this one emerging, I didn't want to miss even the faint chance. Every couple of minutes the earth stirred and erupted, and the molehillock grew towards respectable molehill size.

A tractor growled by in a higher field a hundred yards away, towing a load of silage. If the driver noticed a shabby figure, bent over peering at the ground, perhaps he thought nothing of it. But he might have been a little puzzled, passing and repassing three times in the next half-hour, to see the same immobile figure in the same attitude. 'Typical townie,' he probably said to himself. 'Thinks he's going to see a mole. Give himself backache, more like.'

Once or twice I brushed some earth away, to see exactly where the shaft was, and how big. The size of the plug that was pushed up after that gave me some idea of how small the mole was, and how far down – four inches or more. It would presumably be deeper than usual in this cold weather, with the surface frozen hard. Eventually I decided I was too cold, stiff, and hungry to give Mole any more time to show himself, and headed off, restoring circulation by degrees.

A pair of wrens caught my eye, fluttering around and through clumps of gorse – which were in flower, though not profusely. They say that when the gorse is in flower, it's the season for love, and these wrens certainly seemed in a very close and meaningful relationship, chattering together, watching one another and staying close. It was heart-warming to watch, and I still needed warming, so kept going, soon arriving at a signpost and steps up to a railway embankment.

The signpost indicated that here the Staffordshire Way left the other two trails and ascended the steps, which had been built by the West Midlands Conservation Corps. The railway was once the Churnet Valley line, a major branch of the North Staffordshire; almost a secondary main line rather than a branch, and in LMS days was worked by big brisk Fowler or Stanier 2-6-4 tanks. These were outstanding locomotives, popular with enginemen who appreciated their speed, strength, and smooth running, as one former fireman reports:

> Perhaps their remarkably quiet, stable ride, free from fuss and trauma was the most notable aspect of these excellent engines. Certainly they produced a very crisp healthy bark when getting under way or when pushed on banks, but at normal running speeds with the cut-off at around 15-20%, only a soft sibilant purr emanated from the chimney.[1]

The old NSR had nothing as big as the 2-6-4Ts, but their powerful 0-6-2 and 0-6-4 tanks (left) coped well enough with the busy local traffic in pre-grouping days. The line carried more than local traffic, however; there were through freight trains passing by night, and excursions by day.

[1] Essery, *op cit*

Some were bringing tourists to Rudyard Lake or Alton Towers, but others were long-distance trains: from Liverpool to Cromer, for example, or Nelson to Bournemouth; and a trainspotter between the wars might have seen ex-Midland or ex-L&Y 0-6-0s, or ex-LNW Precursors, George Vs, Coal Tanks, or Prince of Waleses. Besides these, Crabs, Black Fives, ex-LNW 'Super Ds', and ex-L&Y 2-4-2Ts can all be seen in old photographs.[1]

The Beeching axe was wielded on the basis that a lot of this traffic could go some other way. Yet in the twenty-first century the lack of capacity on the few main lines remaining shows up how useful these secondary lines could have become. With astute marketing and restrained subsidy, the Churnet Valley line could have been kept open, and it would today be keeping a lot of traffic off the roads: there's a handsome station very close to Alton Towers – think how many coach journeys that could have saved.

In some places the railway embankment gave grand views of the hills on both sides of the valley: green below, dusted with white above. Other stretches were enclosed by slim straight trees, which shut out the valley and shut in the walker – a cool quiet corridor, light grey ballast underfoot, light grey cloud overhead, just the occasional bird in the branches: great tits or robins. Ahead was the village of Rushton Spencer, named for the Despencer family, who were Earls of Chester, but held land in this area, to which they would come for the hunting.

Walking along the line of the Knotty, on a long-distance path which also uses the Staffordshire Knot symbol, I came to the Knot Inn (once just called the Railway), where I had planned to have lunch. Approaching, I was suddenly afraid that the pub might be closed; but no, the landlord of the Knot Inn was not Not In, but in; not in Knottin'ley, not in Nottin'ham, not in Nottin' Hill, not insane, not incommunicado, but *in* in the Knot Inn; and I was not insensible of my not inconsiderable good fortune in not instinctively having assumed the Knot Inn would certainly be shut. I am not indifferent, however, to the idea that readers may not entirely appreciate this not inconsiderable number of puns on the Knot Inn; they are therefore not ineluctable, not interminable, and not enforced: readers are not entreated to read through them twice, and hence are not entitled to grumble. Any reader not intending to put up with twenty-eight repetitions of the syllables /notin/ should consider how not English it is to complain about anything.

The symbol of the Staffordshire Knot – which is just a stylised half-hitch, once the badge of the Earls of Stafford, but actually dating from before the Norman Conquest – was set in low relief over the welcoming coal fire, which looked all the better for being flanked by a huge copper coal-scuttle on one side, and a copper kettle on the other, both polished and brilliant.

[1] Jeuda, B (1999) *The Churnet Valley Railway* Lightmoor Press
Jeuda, B (1980) *The Leek, Caldon & Waterhouses Railway* NSR Co Ltd

Copper scuttle and copper kettle: quintessentially English, yet *say* the words, without seeing the comfortingly English spelling, and they sound like a couple of Central American volcanoes. Maybe it was the bright orange flames that made me think of volcanoes; and maybe it was the memory of the earth rolling down the slopes of the erupting molehill. It's still true that it's as much English spelling as the sound of words that gives them their character. Take the name Churchill – what could be more English? Yet spell it the German way: Tschötschil, and it seems an alien, unpronounceable and untrustworthy name. It's equally odd-seeming in Turkish: Çöçil. Who (in England, that is) would have voted for a politician with a name like that?

Brown bread roast beef sandwiches with a generous side salad, and some Boddington's, brought straying thoughts back to reality. Beer, bread and beef went very nicely together: Boddington's has been described by real ale enthusiasts as 'a golden straw-coloured bitter in which the grainy malt, hop and bitter character can be spoiled by a cloying sweetness'. It wasn't sweet today, but generally speaking it isn't one of my absolute favourite beers. Nevertheless, it was disappointing to hear that the Belgian megaconglomerate that bought Boddington's was closing the Strangeways factory, and ceasing production, when beer had been brewed there for well over two hundred years. Now any real ale with a Boddington's label is brewed at Hyde's.

Strengthened and encouraged by lunch, I was ready to go on as far as time would allow, and set myself the northern end of Rudyard Lake as a target, following the Staffordshire Way along the old railway line. It seemed more or less level, but somewhere not far beyond the Knot Inn I crossed the watershed between the Mersey catchment area and that of the Trent. The real whereabouts of the watershed was complicated by a feeder stream, flowing gently under the track, which was actually pinching (from the River Dane) water that ought to have been flowing all the way to Liverpool, and feeding it into Rudyard Lake so that (via the River Churnet and the Caldon Canal) it would end up flowing past Burton, Nottingham, Scunthorpe, and Hull. The ecological implications were mind-boggling: surely you wouldn't be allowed to do that today; but it's been happening for a long time, so the ecosystems of Mersey and Humber must be well-adjusted by now.

Over to the right was the isolated Rushton church, of low and modest dimensions, originally built of wood. The inscription on Thomas Meakyn's gravestone, just outside the church, tells a grim story: this young Rushton lad, born in 1760, went away as a teenager to find work. He found employment as a groom some twenty miles south of here, in Stone, a small town beginning to be prosperous as a result of the new Grand Trunk canal. Thomas began to be a little over-friendly with his employer's daughter, and then suddenly fell ill, and in a short time was buried. It is said, rather implausibly, that one of the horses he had been responsible for kept returning to the grave. Whether because of this, or some other grounds for suspicion, the body was exhumed, and signs were found that the young man had revived and vainly tried to escape from the coffin. His sweetheart's father was a chemist by trade, and had both means and motive to administer drugs to simulate illness and apparent death.

Thomas was reburied in his home village, and his grave marked 'as a man falleth before wicked men, so fell I' – a variation on King David's words in 2 Samuel, lamenting the treacherous and sinister murder of Abner by Joab.

Walking through this valley, I was following the route of the rebel army in December 1745. Lord George Murray, Bonny Prince Charlie's Lieutenant General, was keen to avoid meeting Cumberland in battle, and Cumberland was known to be south of Stoke; so one column had marched towards Congleton, and a cavalry foray was made from there southwards. Colonel Ker, with thirty cavalrymen, patrolled as far as Talke, where they encountered government scouts, capturing one. They were happy to let the others escape to report back that the rebels seemed to be heading for Newcastle-under-Lyme.

Satisfied that Cumberland would be expecting them to advance directly southward, Murray then led his part of the force eastward, early on the morning of December 3rd, close by the Cloud and down through this valley into Leek. The main army followed direct from Macclesfield; and all were well on their way to Derby before Cumberland realised he had been outflanked. The weather then might well have been much the same as this January afternoon: fairly cold unless you kept moving, but good walking weather with occasional watery sunshine.

Up to the left was Gun Hill, where a gallows stood until the 1880s, said to have been where John Naden was gibbeted in 1731, his rotting body swinging in chains for some time thereafter. Naden had supposedly been persuaded to murder his master, Robert Brough, by his master's wife – who returned to the scene of the deed to go through the corpse's pockets and make it look like a simple robbery. However she missed Naden's knife lying nearby. It is said that he was actually executed outside her door.

The level railway track made for brisk walking, and before long I came to the wetlands at the north end of Rudyard Lake. Bare trees stood above stretches of straw-coloured reeds and rushes, with open water beyond.

5th May 2003

It looked quite different, much brighter and greener and less bare, when I returned with Ishbel on a sunny spring Bank Holiday. Showers were forecast, so we took an umbrella – hardly hiking equipment, but we weren't aiming at more than a stroll. We decided to follow the North Staffordshire railway line along the east side of the lake, rather than the Staffordshire Way's route round the west side.

Just at first the lake was out of sight, and we were in a quiet cutting, with the sunlight sifting through the leaves, colour supplied by plentiful bluebells, dandelions, dog violets and wood anemones, and birdsong all around us. We thought we could identify both chiffchaff and willow warbler song. A fine chaffinch posed on a branch just above us, and sang proudly.

As he turned slightly, and as the breeze ruffled his feathers, we saw his puffed-out chest shifting colour from bright pink to buff, and back again. It seemed to be a matter of how the light fell: enough to explain why chaffinches sometimes look exotically coloured, and sometimes quite subdued.

As we moved on we gained a clear view of the lake, waterfowl dotted here and there, a small trimaran making the most of the breeze, and a dinghy with a bright blue spinnaker that startled us with a loud crack as it filled. Rudyard Lake looks wonderfully natural, but is actually artificial, built in 1797 to hold 122 million cubic feet of water and supply it to the Caldon canal. There can be little doubt that this lake enhances the beauty of the valley, with its wooded slopes either side. It would have looked less attractive in 1933, when a drought left it three-quarters empty; but normally the level holds up well.

In September 1864 the tightrope artist Carlos Trower, the 'African Blondin', walked across from one hill to another, 100 feet above the lake; as we walked we tried to guess exactly where this most probably happened. The likeliest spot, where the lake is not too wide and the hills either side are quite steep, seemed to us to be near the Lady of the Lake boathouse, a grand brick structure built out from the far shore. This was designed by William Sugden, a Leek architect, in 1893, and features a white statue in a redbrick niche.

There were a number of other interesting mature boathouses: the lake had clearly been popular for a long time. Captain Webb the channel swimmer, who we last encountered at Hollingworth Lake (see Book One), came here as well to demonstrate his prowess. John Lockwood Kipling (left) met his future wife Alice here at a picnic that their employers had organised: the couple had such fond memories of the lake that they named their son Rudyard.

As we strolled on, we found ourselves walking alongside a very narrow-gauge railway, laid on one side of the old trackbed. The Rudyard Lake Steam Railway was a relatively new venture; the gauge was 10¼ inches, so it was better described as a miniature railway rather than narrow-gauge. After a while, a tiny Emmett-like loco – tall thin funnel and high spindly cab – wheezed towards us, hauling a rake of open coaches just wide enough for a slim adult and a small child to sit side by side. Minute as the gauge was, at least the engine driver and passengers could sit inside, rather than on, the vehicles. We decided to walk a little further, since we would be able to take the train part of the way back.

At the foot of the lake, by the dam, we saw the steam launch *Lady Alice* waiting for customers. She was a lady of indeterminate age, the hull being a 1953 lifeboat, while the steam engine that propelled her was over a hundred years old, incorporating a sixty-year-old boiler. Such stately maturity suggests a waltz rather than a lively hornpipe, so here is the Steamboat Hornpipe recast as a waltz, an idea Bernard Cromarty once had.

The Steamboat Waltz

We decided there was no time for a cruise, but enjoyed looking round a small exhibition centre, as well as finding basic refreshment in the form of bacon butties. I remember once hearing a folk song in praise of 'the humble bacon butty', complete with every possible rhyme for 'butty' in the entire English language, but I don't have the words, I'm afraid.

Below the dam we located the continuation of the Staffordshire Way, along the canal feeder. There were vivid yellow marsh marigolds with big kidney-shaped leaves growing in the marshes near the path, and we saw a bright orange-tip butterfly as well. The path by the leat was shaded by mature trees, and great tits and a wren fluttered close enough to allow us a good look at their markings. Paddling along in the water was a creamy-grey-coloured drake with a brown head. He seemed to answer the description of a wigeon in some respects, but we didn't see the yellow forehead you would expect; nor, on the other hand, did he have the black chest of a pochard. He didn't seem nervous – we were quite close – so I asked him 'Are you a wigeon?' But this appeared to be an embarrassing question, for he turned away and muttered to himself. Perhaps he was a cross-breed, *anas bassettii* rather than *anas penelope*. On the other hand, perhaps he was actually she, a goldeneye duck rather than a drake of any kind?

Before long we came to the road that took us a short distance to the terminus of the Rudyard Lake Steam Railway, where we packed ourselves into our seats along with a number of families, and watched *Excalibur* run round its train, pausing to take on water. A youngster was earnestly telling his father that the engine was having a *big* drink because it had been working hard and was *very* thirsty. We noticed the plate that said *Excalibur* had come from the Exmoor Steam Railway: recently rebuilt, the driver told me, with more power and a roomier cab.

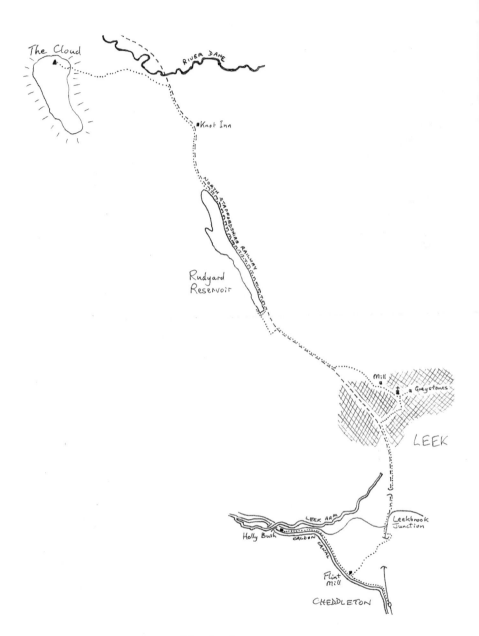

Map for chapters 6 - 8

66

Seven: Rudyard to Leekbrook Junction *(4 miles)*

Colours of winter – Buy Broom Besoms – Brindley's Mill unvisited – compulsory scruffiness – Arts and Crafts – the Greystones Waltz – 2 whales in a mini – portly bishops – tunnelwalking

14th *January 2005*

Returning to Rudyard to continue the walk, well over a year and a half since we had reached that spot, felt quite strange and discontinuous. There was some excuse for the break: during 2003-4 we were teaching in Bosnia. Getting ready to go, not to mention getting straight after returning, gave little opportunity for rambling. In addition we returned to a very wet autumn, and even when it wasn't raining, there were various tasks to catch up on at home. Any time available for the Four Points Ramble went on revising Books One and Two.

But I had missed the walking; at the same time having some doubts about the whole project: whether it was achievable, whether it was a sensible use of time, and whether anyone would really want to read all about it. For so long Rudyard had been the end of the solid red line (everything walked to this point) on the sketch map. It was high time to make some progress on the ground, and finally there came a day when the weather forecaster seemed confident it would stay dry.

On the way south, a few landmarks served as reminders of the walk so far: the curious single-turreted tower of North Rode church; Bosley Locks (where some serious heavy maintenance seemed to be under way); the Cloud (looking appropriately hazy as it had done on another winter's day two years ago); an advertising board for the Knot Inn; and Rudyard Lake, flanked by green slopes with bare trees casting long shadows.

By the time I set out walking along the railway embankment, once again following the Knotty's Churnet Valley line, the sense of time-lag was diminishing, and the awareness of the hundred or more miles of footpath behind me, and uncounted hundreds of miles ahead, as a continuous route, was increasing. The going was firm, the weather cold enough to encourage brisk walking. The embankment was fringed by many small trees, silver birches prominent; in the summer it might feel quite enclosed, but now the trees were bare enough for there to be a clear view of the valley on either side. A thin film of ice covered parts of the ponds below. Blackbirds and magpies came and went, as did many small brown birds with piping voices, generally just far enough away to be unidentifiable, for the rambler ignorant of the fine specific details of birdsong.

Further on, the line plunged into a cutting which might have been a blaze of colour in another season; but now neither broom nor heather was in flower; and the dead fronds of fern and bracken had faded from autumn russet into dull brown. At first glance it could have been called drab, yet on steady contemplation some of the grasses and mosses were a strong green, and the range of greens, browns, greys and buffs was rich and subtle, more varied than any commercial paint colour-chart, with its dozens of pretentiously-named shades. The more I looked, the more beautiful the cutting became.

Emerging from the cutting onto another embankment, I was surrounded by dry broom bushes, and the old song began running through my head:

If ye want a besom for to sweep your hoose
Come to me, my hinny, ye may have your choose

Chorus: Buy broom besoms, buy them when they're new
Fine heather bred uns, better never grew.

Besoms for a penny, rangers for a plack
If ye will not buy I'll tie them on my back ... *Chorus*

If I had a horse then I would have a cart;
If I had a wife she would take my part. ... *Chorus*

Had I but a wife I care not what she be-
If she's but a woman that's enough for me ... *Chorus*

Before long the map indicated that the shortest path to Leek lay down the embankment, over a stile, and through a sea of mud in contrasting shades of vermilion and chocolate. Fortunately the weather was cold enough for the mud to be fairly firm; though once the worst of the morass had been safely traversed, the lush grass in the next field turned out to be rather softer. Deep cloven-hoofed pits showed where cows had been standing about and sinking into the ground.

Some of the gorse on a neighbouring hillside was in flower: it was good to know the kissing season wasn't over. Before long the footpath came to an end by a line of stately mature trees, behind a substantial brick house with a superb view down the valley. Emerging through the gate onto the main road, I was buffeted by the slipstream of a huge articulated tanker bound for Broughty Ferry in Scotland. The walk along the main road into the centre of Leek was less picturesque than the path so far, but still interesting. Substantial industries (chemical, and agricultural machinery, among others) gave clues to Leek's present prosperity. Leek Town's stadium gave no indication of what the next home match would be, but seemed in good order for this modest level of football. Soon on the left was Brindley's Mill with its associated museum – closed at this time of year; we'll have to come back and see it. (Three further attempts to visit Brindley's Mill were also abortive: we don't seem to have the knack of coming to Leek when it's open. Meanwhile we've seen many canal structures and various mills constructed by this industrious industrial genius, and learned something of his life through reading up the histories of the early canals. But it would still be nice to see the inside of this humble but solid cornmill, built in 1752, and to see artefacts such as the surveyor's level that Brindley used.)

On the other side of the road was a building that had not only been a chapel but also a Ragged School: inspired title, an encouragement to small boys everywhere. Imagine a school where you're *supposed* to be scruffy; where smartness might lead to a detention; where you could get lines for tucking your shirt in, or caned for combing your hair! I could have thriven there.[1]

John Pounds, the Portsmouth *tutor*, and founder of Ragged Schools.

Further up on the right was a vast and shabby mill building: not quite derelict: most of the windows had glass in, and there were a few indications of occupation and activity. Big Mill, as it was bluntly known, had been where Wardle and Davenport carried on their silk weaving and dyeing business. Leek built its prosperity on silk, particularly on silk dyeing: a very fine black dye was achieved locally, which became fashionable in the years of Queen Victoria's mourning. Later, William Morris (below), the artist, writer and designer, came here to experiment with vegetable dyes and silk printing, and developed famous patterns such as Trellis, Vine, Pimpernel, Chrysanthemum and Marigold. His dream was to make the ordinary essential objects found in every town and every home both durable and beautiful:

> That art will make our streets as beautiful as the woods, as elevating as the mountain-sides: it will be a pleasure and a rest, and not a weight upon the spirits to come from the open country into a town; every man's house will be fair and decent, soothing to his mind and helpful to his work: all the works of man that we live amongst and handle will be in harmony with nature, will be reasonable and beautiful...[2]

It was one thing to decide that everything should be beautiful, and quite another to determine what beauty actually was. Morris had very clear views on this, as on most things. For him, beauty was found in the unknown or uncertain; things should not be totally comprehended at first glance. As with his late prose romances, the charm was in the unexplained – yet vividly delineated – detail:

[1] Yes, I do know what Ragged Schools really were. Ishbel thinks my readers will think I'm ignorant. They were free schools for poor children: I had thought that Thomas Guthrie started the idea, but he was picking up on the crippled shoemaker John Pounds's 1818 initiative in Portsmouth.
[2] Morris, W (1877) *The Lesser Arts*

In all patterns which are meant to fill the eye and satisfy the mind, there should be a certain mystery. We should not be able to read the whole thing at once, nor desire to do so, nor be impelled by that desire to go on tracing line after line to find out how the pattern is made...[1]

Leek was by no means a 'weight upon the spirits', but it was not quite Morris's earthly paradise

either. The stonework of Big Mill was dark green from damp, and the red brick darkened by age. A pigeon flew to one of the few missing panes and disappeared into the blackness inside.

Meanwhile the road wound upwards in a deepening canyon, out of which a flight of steps led so that you could walk above the canyon rather than in the depths. The steps were carpeted with beech-mast, and the pathway above covered in thick green moss. Coming nearer to the centre of Leek, the architecture became intriguing: a tiny octagonal public convenience squeezed in the angle of a hairpin junction, more of Sugden's work; the dark stone of the eighteenth-century Old Grammar School (now a Scout headquarters); beside that, Petty France, the French quarter; and some fine windows in the Vicarage next to St. Edward's church.

Petty France was where prisoners of war were billeted in Napoleonic times; a significant number liked the town and stayed, even when they could have returned to their homeland. Down where I come from, Napoleonic prisoners were put in Dartmoor Prison; few stayed in that bleak and misty spot any longer than they had to.

But Leek has charm, particularly St. Edward the Confessor's, dating from the thirteenth century, and including features from most periods since. Like many old churches, it was extensively renovated in Victorian times, though more tastefully than usual, since William Morris was heavily involved. His influence can be seen in the stained glass and in the embroidery, produced by the Leek School of Embroidery, founded by Elizabeth Wardle with Morris's encouragement. He was particularly enthusiastic about any skilled handicraft, seeing it as a counterbalance to the growth of mass-production techniques in the Industrial Revolution, and the whole Arts and Crafts movement promoted this approach, valuing the contribution of the skilled craftsman to Art.

Leek was a good place to find craftsmen; a town full of independent, individualistic, hard-working folk who preferred to be their own bosses. It is said that this native independence was encouraged by the dissolution of Dieulacres Abbey (just

[1] Morris, W (1881) *Some Hints on Pattern-Designing*

north of here) in 1538. Elsewhere the Church lands were often kept as large estates by grand landowners; here on the edge of the Staffordshire moorlands Sir Ralph Bagnall decided to parcel up the land into small holdings that local men could afford, and sold to many farmers who had no pretensions beyond their own independence.

A little further on was the Greystones tea room in a handsome seventeenth-century building. This was once the home of Joshua Nicholson, a silk manufacturer, and still looks more like a private residence than a tearoom. Beyond and behind Greystones rose the copper-capped tower of the Nicholson Institute (see the drawing on page 3). The Institute, built by Sugden and Son, was given to the town as an art gallery and museum, and was set back from the road, out of respect for the beauty of the older building. The Sugdens, William the father and son Larner, were responsible for many of Leek's finest Victorian buildings, adding a measure of grandeur to the numerous interesting older buildings in the town. Larner Sugden was contemporary with William Morris, and joined him in forming the Society for the Preservation of Ancient Buildings, which found plenty of scope in Leek.

The Greystones Waltz *(specially for the E whistle)*

The Greystones Tea Room was just a front room, and quite busy; but there was a tiny table in the corner where one person could rest their back against the wall, so there was no need to feel bad about taking a table on my own. Having ordered tea and toasted teacake, I could relax and look around. The clientele all seemed to be older than me, which was refreshing: I'm not often the youngest these days. The walls were covered in paintings for sale; and gilt clocks seemed to be a feature. The waiter (also the proprietor) was in unhurried perpetual motion, dapper in waistcoat and red bow tie, chatting to the customers (and he seemed to know most of them) and cracking jokes. 'How do you get two whales in a mini?' he was asking an elderly lady at the next table. The joke was about the right vintage for the gathering: I first remember hearing it nearly forty years ago. It was funnier this time because the lady didn't get it at all, even after three or four attempts at explanation.

As I was preparing to leave, the proprietor asked me if I was walking, and on finding where I was headed gave good directions for the most direct route to Cheddleton. (When I reappeared at lunchtime he was gratifyingly surprised that I'd been there and back in the time – but for a busy waiter, time probably whizzes by).

71

The route through the town centre took in the cobbled square, where on another day Ishbel and I enjoyed the market stalls, and she got some remarkably cheap sandals (blessings on King John's 1207 charter). By the square was the Butter Market, with its covered kiosks, and everything from cheese to second-hand books; and many more interesting buildings. An old pub called the Wilkes' Head, when later checked out, turned out to be a simple and truly unspoilt place. The regulars clearly appreciated the basic and old-fashioned décor: 'I love a scruffy pub', said one, 'it's like a haven for me – there's always someone to talk to'.

An even older pub, the early seventeenth century Roebuck in Derby Street, served us some fine Staffordshire oatcakes on yet another visit to Leek. Ishbel and I like oatcakes anyway, but they taste the better for not being available all round the country. There's little enough regional food left, as menus merge into a global standard; we'll always go for anything local or home-made.

The Hon. John Byng was in Leek in 1792; having ridden over from Macclesfield, he put up at the George, found his room, and the supper, to his liking, successfully collected letters from the Post Office, bought a riding whip at the market, and was well content with life: '-- My landlord was the most ignorant of the ignorant! This was the finest day I have met with; - and the moon shone brightly in the evening.'[1] Presumably Byng was so satisfied with life at that point that his landlord's ignorance seemed entertaining rather than irritating.

Down St. Edward Street stood a succession of fine and varied buildings, some designed by Sugden in the Arts and Crafts style, others older and equally impressive. Up the hill beyond stood All Saints, the spacious Arts and Crafts church which so impressed John Betjeman. We were there once for an early music concert, and were less impressed by finding standing room only: large as the church was, the organisers had managed to sell more tickets than they had provided seats. Nonetheless we did appreciate the breadth and balance of the architecture.

A less remarkable landmark on my route was Safeways, which was on the site of Leek's old railway station. There were some interesting tall Edwardian brick chimneys on a house nearby, but Safeways itself looked like nothing much, other than lots of other Safeways, and there was little to recall the busy station and goods yard that had once served the town.

Beyond the car park the beginning of the footpath along the track of the old railway appeared, among very ugly surroundings: building sites, a chemical works, and warehouse yards, with scrubby leafless hawthorns on one side of the path and tall grey galvanised iron palings on the other. In this grubby, bleak and bare environment appeared first a wren, very close so that I could study its barred brown markings; then a perky little dunnock, streaky brown and grey, another bird that you see less in summer because of its liking for thick undergrowth; then a chaffinch, colourful among the dark tangled thorn branches; and then four bullfinches with their black caps, and two of them with puffed-out chests resplendent in ecclesiastical red-purple.

---

[1] Andrews, *op cit*

72

Dompfaff, the Germans call a bullfinch, the cathedral preacher; the Swedes make it *Domherre,* the lord of the cathedral, gently hinting that portly bishops in episcopal attire, perched in tall pulpits, look like self-important little birds.

After a little, the path emerged from its passage through the industrial estates, and ran along a high embankment between a well-managed golf course on one side, and contrastingly unspoilt countryside on the other: even the colour of the grass was quite different. A silent thrush scuttered under some deep red dogwood stems at the side of the track; and a little flock of long-tailed tits flitted through the branches above. Further on, the old railway ran through a tunnel under a little hill, which looked very like a child's first model railway, where a hill with a tunnel appears in isolation on a flat baseboard. So here the hill looked so small that one wondered why the North Staffordshire hadn't gone round it rather than through it. Birchall Tunnel was dry, high and wide, with a good view and clear daylight all the way through its 69 yards. Not at all like some disused railway tunnels; despite the dissimilarities, I was reminded of New Year House Parties on the Isle of Wight in the late sixties, when as a group we took the chance to walk through the long tunnel (then recently closed to rail traffic) under Boniface Down to Ventnor. Mary Hopkin's *Those were the Days* was in the hit parade at the time, so we sang in celebration:

> Those were the days, my friends; the tunnel never ends,
> It's long and dark, and dank and wet inside;
> The bats fly round and round, there's potholes in the ground,
> But never fear, for Fullerton's our guide!

After forty years, only the chorus sticks in memory now; Nigel Richardson's inventive verses have gone. What you hear, you forget; what you sing, you remember.

Leaving the tunnel, voices, panting, and running feet sounded close behind: half turning, I saw that the joggers were still two hundred yards away beyond the other end of the tunnel, which was acting as a giant megaphone to funnel the sound in my direction (helped perhaps by the northerly breeze). They were a fit couple, those joggers, carrying on a conversation as they came, and greeting me as they passed. Incidentally, every one of the ten or so other walkers I met that day exchanged a greeting: English people aren't all reserved.

Not far beyond the tunnel the path passed buffers, and soon rails were in place, though clearly nothing had run on them for years: the tufts of coarse grass and little thorn bushes growing between the sleepers proved that. To the left was a small wood of young slender trees that had grown up over a set of sidings, leaving rusting rails running spookily through woodland; ahead were straight tracks heading directly into the low midday winter sun, so that, rusty as they were, they gleamed palely in converging perspective, leading the eye into the hazy distance. The path appeared as a dark wobbly line between the rails, a reminder that I was walking south, on a path that would eventually take me to the southernmost point in England.

Eight: Leekbrook Junction to the Holly Bush *(3 miles)*

Yankee consolidation – mole population control – Molecatcher's Hornpipe – grinding flints – Darwin's gay teapot – The Dusty Miller – minimising risk – delicious spring – olfactory memory – the acorn-eating chatterbox

14th January 2005

At the end of the straight, the rails came to a junction, presided over by a tall and dilapidated North Staffordshire signalbox, with its characteristic steep pitched roof and sharp finials. Once a signalman here would have seen plenty of action, with passenger trains to and from Uttoxeter via Leek crossing the path of mineral trains from Caldon Low quarries to Stoke, and returning empties. The track from Caldon Low (which had seen traffic till fairly recently, and was now mothballed rather than irreversibly closed) curved down and in from my left, and then immediately veered off to the right towards Stoke. I could imagine the lean taper boiler and low-slung cylinders of a grimy Stanier 8F, as it eased a rake of loaded wagons down the slope to the junction, perhaps at little more than walking pace; then the slow bark of the exhaust, the squeal of wheel flanges on the curve, and the clank of loose couplings as the driver picked up pace once through the points.

The 8F was Stanier's modernisation and development of the first taper boiler 2-8-0, which Churchward had introduced on the Great Western as early as 1903. Even the GW enginemen were happy with the 8F, once they realised its quality and inspiration. 'When we left her on the ash road it was the end of a perfect day,' wrote Harold Gasson enthusiastically of the experience of firing an 8F for the first time.[1] LMS enginemen were equally impressed with their new heavy freight loco, which 'instilled a high degree of confidence in their crews since they tended to flatter the less skilled while…allowing exceptional performance to be extracted by the proficient'.[2]

Although the Caldon Low track was still in place, recalling memories of past freight, there had once been much more than this at the junction. The north to east curve, the engine shed and railway cottages, the interchange platform for the electric tramway to the County Mental Hospital, were all now gone, leaving the junction looking quieter and more deserted than it would once have been; the huge Dye Works nearby had also disappeared. Beyond the junction were rails fenced off and still in use: the northern end of the preserved Churnet Valley Railway. The footpath turned aside and wound its way through trees before crossing over the restored line, with signs warning the walker to Stop, Look, and Listen, and Beware of Trains. There was nothing running that day, and little to see apart from a clear view all the way through the short and straight Cheddleton Tunnel.

(A couple of years later, Ishbel and I managed to be passing just as a large and rugged American 2-8-0, uttering its characteristic deep drawn-out whistle, brought a train of holidaymakers through Leekbrook tunnel and then ran round and buffered up

[1] Gasson, H (2005) 'The greatest engine ever built at Swindon' *Steam World*, June 2005
[2] Essery, *op cit*

at the south end ready to head back to Cheddleton. This was a different 2-8-0 to the Stanier model I'd imagined passing through Leekbrook before. The 8F would have looked long and lanky, muscular but spare; while this Yankee S160 was built like a buffalo, all bulk and brawn, with a huge boiler and cylinders.

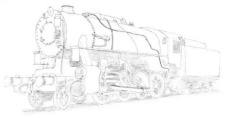

The guard came and manned the crossing, and was able to tell us about the locomotive. It had been built in Ohio, he said, small by American standards in order to go anywhere in Europe during the Second World War. Locos of that type were seen in numbers in England in 1943/4, during the logistical build-up to D-day. But this particular example, it seemed, had been built too late to cross the Atlantic and serve in the war, and had instead been sold direct to China, where it had pulled coal trains up until the 1990s. Eventually redundant in China, it had been purchased by enthusiasts, brought to England for the first time, and restored to pristine condition in the 21st century.)

Beyond the crossing, the track led to the main road; and I had to walk roadside as far as Cheddleton. At least there was a pavement. The road went up a hill that was home to some moles that were either very numerous or very industrious: fields were packed with molehills, and even tiny strips of roadside verge had their row of brown humps. Maybe there had been a population explosion since miners stopped wearing moleskin trousers.

Later I saw a newspaper article where a professional molecatcher bemoaned the shortage of strychnine, which was forcing him to revert to more traditional molecatch-ing methods. He had the skills, but the extra time needed to liquidate the same number of moles meant charging the farmers far higher rates; and in the current state of the agricultural economy they would rather suffer the moles than part with that much cash, so he wasn't getting much work. Strychnine would soon be illegal anyway, it seemed; the molecatcher had a conspiracy theory, suspecting a pro-mole mole in the Department for Rural Affairs.

The poet John Clare would have rejoiced that moles were being less persecuted; he had a particular love for those furry little tunnelers, and hated to see their corpses displayed:

> …I leave a sigh behind
> While I see the little mouldywharps hang sweeing to the wind
> On the only aged willow that in all the field remains
> And nature hides her face where they're sweeing in their chains
> And in a silent murmuring complains.[1]

Molecatchers naturally have a bad reputation with animal lovers; Mary Russell Mitford describes the dark, dour and cadaverous Isaac Bint with a ghoulish relish in the appropriacy of his grim exterior to his murderous trade:

> The stride is awful: he hath the stalk of a ghost … his clothes, hands, and face are of the colour of the mould in which he delves. The little round traps which hang behind him over one shoulder, as well as the strings of dead moles which embellish the other, are incrusted with dirt like a tombstone; and the staff which he plunges into the little hillocks, by which he traces the course of his small quarry, returns a hollow sound, as if tapping on the lid of a coffin.[2]

But later in the story Isaac turns out to have a hidden well of loving-kindness which gives life rather than death, and is called 'our good molecatcher', though that does not suggest anything as jolly as the following traditional tune. It's an old 3/2 hornpipe, and I've altered the key of the middle section so that the whole tune is playable on the A whistle.

The Molecatcher's Hornpipe

Finally I reached the bridge over the Churnet, the focal point of a scenic valley that had also pleased the Honorable John Byng in 1792: '…the view of the bridge, navigation, and church, compose a most happy scenery,' he wrote. The Caldon Canal was relatively new in Byng's day, but mature enough to have integrated into the landscape. I leaned on the parapet, looking at the flint mill, and remembered the last time I'd been there, which didn't feel like seven, nearly eight years earlier.

---

[1] Clare, J 'Remembrances'
[2] Mitford, MR (1824-32) *Our Village*

We had first visited Cheddleton Flint Mill with my youngest nephew, who was then in his first year at Staffordshire University. The mill made a convenient destination, and Tony had some interest in history – indeed he was supposed to be studying it, along with Spanish – so we checked out the museum, with its two huge undershot waterwheels, and its chert grindstones. Flint was used in earthenware, but grinding the flint to powder was dreadful for the lungs of those who worked in the flint mills; so in 1726 a certain Thomas Benson patented a method of grinding the flint underwater; a method that, thirty years or so later, was improved by the ingenious Brindley, who probably built the less ancient of the twin mills at Cheddleton.

The various exhibits gave the beginnings of an idea of the whole process of pottery manufacture, which we later filled out with visits to other museums and potteries, so that in the end we knew somewhat more than we had done; but it remained to us a craft full of mysteries, with its specialised meanings given to familiar words, terse and blunt: *slip, slop, bat, pug, bung, fettle, muffle,* or *crank,* as well as trade-specific or dialect terms: *mawl, bont, blunge, saggar, glost, clammins,* and *hoss.* Job titles were equally mysterious and arcane: *cod placers, drab pressers, cockspur makers, thimble pickers, wedgers, jiggerers, jollyers, mouldrunners, sliphousemen, groundlayers, saggar makers,* and at the bottom of the hierarchy, the young and humble *saggar maker's bottom knockers* (right). A basic description of the craft of pottery was once given in verse by Erasmus
Darwin, starting in his leisurely way far back in time:

> Hence ductile clays in wide expansion spread,
> Soft as the Cygnet's down, their snow-white bed;
> With yielding flakes successive forms reveal,
> And change obedient to the whirling wheel.
> First China's sons, with early art elate,
> Formed the gay tea-pot, and the pictured plate;
> Saw with illumined brow and dazzled eyes
> In the red stove vitrescent colours rise;
> Specked her tall beakers with enamelled stars,
> Her monster-josses, and gigantic jars;
> Smeared her huge dragons with metallic hues,
> With golden purples, and cobaltic blues;
> Bade on wide hills her porcelain castles glare,
> And glazed Pagodas tremble in the air.

Darwin wrote huge quantities of this kind of poetry; it must have come to him almost as easily as prose does to lesser mortals. He continued his history of pottery by way of Etruria, and since I was aiming to walk through there in a few miles' time, I could look forward to picking it up there. I was well prepared to find out as much as possible about pottery; as J.B. Priestley wrote: 'unless you are prepared to take a deep and lasting interest in what happens inside those ovens, it would be better for you to take the first train anywhere'.[1]

Outside the mill were the kilns where the flint was calcined, that is, baked or roasted for days on end so that it became brittle enough to be easily broken up and ground by the huge chert stones. The kilns were right beside the canal so that flint could be brought by water and unloaded straight into the kiln; in fact this traffic in flint was one of the reasons for building the Caldon Canal in the 1770s. Raw flint came up the canal from the Trent & Mersey; and ground flint went back down to the potteries in Stoke. The other reason was the limestone from the quarries at Caldon Low, which needed an outlet to the wider world via the Trent & Mersey. This would have been a bustling place once; and dusty, too, despite the improvements of Brindley's submerged grinding process. The following is one of the best known of the old English 3/2 hornpipes; the bass line has been added for a low G whistle. We follow this tune with the *Cobbler's Hornpipe* and the *Hare's Maggot*, which will appear in Book 4 of the Four Points Ramble.

The Dusty Miller

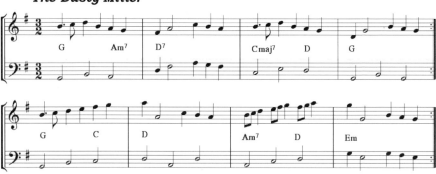

Near the kilns was moored the restored narrowboat *Vienna*, in its Fellows, Morton & Clayton livery. Within a few years in the 1960s and 70s, the mills, the boat, and the canal had all been restored, although the Caldon Canal took considerably longer to rescue from closure, and restore to navigation, than it had taken to survey and build two hundred years earlier. Nevertheless, thanks to the patience and persistence of a few determined folk, it was done, and now aunt, uncle and nephew decided to make the most of some pleasant weather and walk the towpath.

As we strolled along the Caldon canal, the proximity of water took Tony onto the topic of canoeing, and he expounded the joys of waterways rather less placid than the stretch beside us: the Upper Dart, for example, with its huge granite boulders: crack your head on one as you capsize, and it won't matter how clever your technique is, because you won't be conscious to remember to use it. He was talking quite responsibly, as he saw it, of the challenge of minimising risk; but of course there had to be a fair degree of risk for there to be any challenge in working out how to minimise

[1] Priestley, JB (1933) *English Journey*

it. To our middle-aged ears it sounded as if he was detailing quite a lot of ways in which he could die young: not something we would really want to happen.

6th April 2007

Ten years later, he was still alive; but now he was an officer in the Gurkhas, and had expanded the risks that he enjoyed 'minimising' to include deadly cobras in the Borneo jungle, crossfire in the mountains of Afghanistan, rickety rope bridges in Nepal, landmines in Bosnia, nasty tropical infections from Belize, and no doubt many others that he didn't tell us about. Just thinking about all the danger, turbulence, and potential violence in the world emphasised the peacefulness of this corner of the Staffordshire countryside, as Ishbel and I returned to the point that we had strolled to with our young nephew in the previous millennium.

This time I was keen to see the Churnet Valley Railway in action, and we walked down the towpath to Cheddleton station, passing a narrowboat that was selling paintings and sketches. The weather was warm and sunny, and the lesser celandines made a carpet of yellow stars under the trees. Horse chestnut leaves were just emerging: still drooping rather than fully splayed. A peacock butterfly wafted by and posed on the towpath; we also saw Small Tortoiseshells and a few bumble bees. It was the best of spring, with everything awakening and the promise of much more to come. 'Oh to be in England,' wrote Robert Browning, 'now that April's here!' We were in England, and it was delicious.

The station proved to be an elegant stone building of classic North Staffordshire Railway design, with tall angular chimneys. We sat in a shed opposite and drank coffee as we waited for the train. The interior of the shed was more interesting than the plain exterior: there were old prints and posters to evoke the days of steam, and I hoped soon to see and hear and smell real steam, that powerful reminder of the past.

Before too long a whistle sounded and a smart Standard 4 tank brought its train in – very much the sort of locomotive that would have run this line in the 1950s – and the smell of coalsmoke, lubricating oil, and hot metal was exactly as it should be. All that was lacking was the shining rose madder livery of the old Knotty.

Later we enjoyed the cosiness of the Boat Inn, on the far side of the canal, serving savoury Staffordshire oatcake with cheese and tomato, washed down by Marston's Burton bitter. We chose oatcakes for the chance to eat something that isn't available in every corner of England; regional specialities either seem to disappear, or to be marketed all over the country. We haven't yet been able to detect the difference between Staffordshire and Derbyshire oatcakes, but we'll keep trying.

21st March 2005

We had walked the towpath north-westwards from the flint mill just over two years earlier. That was a mild equinocturnal day, with every hint of spring: green leaves just beginning to burgeon from elder branches; daffodils in full flower along the towpath, and birdsong all around. Yet most of the trees and bushes were still bare and the canal commanded a wider view of its surroundings: the wooded hillside to the left and the wide expanse of swamp and reeds, below to the right, where the Churnet met the Endon Brook. We sat on a convenient bench and watched a blue narrowboat, *Misty Waters II*, chug gently by, with a friendly greeting from the steersman. Before long *Sojourn* passed us in the opposite direction. It was good to see boats on the move again, brought out by the warmer weather and the Easter break.

As we moved on, the canal curved westwards, under slopes of dark holly and ivy, with here and there red boles of Scots pine contrasting with glossy green holly. A chaffinch flew across the canal, bright in pink and grey, its white wing flashes sharply marked. Not long afterwards, a jay did likewise, and perched among bare branches, where he could be admired as he preened his fine feathers of black, white, cinnamon and sky-blue. When very young, I used to take home the little blue feathers that caught the eye in woodland, but I don't recall such a good view of a living bird: they used to be shyer.

Linnaeus called the Jay *garrulus glandarius*, the acorn-eating chatterbox. Bewick tells of the antics of domesticated jays that were accomplished mimics:

> We have heard one imitate the sound of a saw so exactly, that though it was on a Sunday, we could hardly be persuaded that there was not a carpenter at work in the house. Another, at the approach of cattle, had learned to hound a cur dog upon them, by whistling and calling his name: at last, during frost, the dog was excited to attack a cow big with calf, when the animal fell on the ice, and was hurt: the Jay was complained of as a nuisance, and its owner was obliged to destroy it.[1]

Our jay did nothing so dramatic, but eventually flew off, flashing blue and white as it went. Walking on, we passed the pleasant-looking wooded valley of Deep Hayes, a country park managed by Staffordshire Council; and twice I heard the yelping laugh of a green woodpecker, but didn't see anything. Along the canal narrowboats were moored here and there, some names memorable and others intriguing: *Slim Chance, Tamarack,* and *Gondolier's Moon*; *Andicy* and *Welvaren.* We couldn't help wondering where the names came from and whether they had any special meaning. It seemed a fair guess that *Andicy* might be owned by Andrew, Diana, and Cynthia; but there might have been some completely different etymology.

Across the valley, and halfway up the hillside opposite, the pale green super-structure of a narrowboat could be seen as it navigated the Leek Arm. It was a slightly bizarre sight, for the canal itself was invisible, hugging the contour so closely that the boat appeared to be moving through a field like a cardboard cutout in a primitive animation. At our own, lower level, we came round a bend to the Holly Bush Inn, where I had started to walk two months before. Having now filled in the little gap in the Four Points Ramble, we retired to the black-beamed, brass- and copper-garnished, and fire-brightened interior, to take tea (for the driver) and cider (for the passenger).

[1] Bewick, *op cit*

80

Nine: The Holly Bush to Burslem *(8 miles)*

Jacob's Ladder – death of Brindley –outsize poultry – floating hedgehogs – litter reserve – Tufted Ducks – flat cap march – danger for slow walkers – the Loop Line

24th January 2005

I returned to the Caldon canal on a cold, but dry Monday morning, wrapped up well against a chilly north wind. As I set off, the mournful braying of a donkey echoed across the valley; a moment later two friendly donkeys came up to the drystone wall and greeted me. It was a nice start to the day.

I joined the main line of the canal by the Holly Bush Inn and got into a brisk stride, to counter the effects of the wind. Across the canal was moored *Watersnail* of Stourbridge, which had presumably come up the Staffordshire and Worcestershire canal from beyond the other end of the county. Between the Caldon, Trent & Mersey, Shropshire Union, Wyrley & Essington, Coventry, and Staffs & Worcs Canals, it is claimed that Staffordshire has more miles of canals than any other English county. By the time I got out of Staffordshire, I would have walked quite a few of them.

I went under the aqueduct carrying the Leek Arm without really taking in what it was; once there had been a staircase of three locks here, but then three new separate locks were constructed further west, and the aqueduct allowed the lower level of the main line to pass under the Leek Arm. Although I missed this, I did admire the new (only 165 years old) Hazelhurst Locks, and the fine cast iron bridge carrying the towpath onto the Leek Arm.

Round another bend was moored a long green narrowboat with the evocative name *Jacob's Ladder* – immediately suggesting all sorts of associations. The boat's owners may have named it for a rope ladder with wooden rungs: such a one as my father hung from an apple tree in our back garden fifty years ago; or perhaps they were thinking of the ornamental herb *Polemoneum coeruleum*, with its small blue flowers and clusters of laddered leaves. A Jacob's Ladder could also be a type of grain elevator used in breweries, a development of the ancient bucket lift. But the biblical Jacob dreamed of 'a stairway resting on the earth, with its top reaching to heaven, and the angels of God were ascending and descending on it'. He was afraid, thinking 'surely the Lord is in this place, and I was not aware of it. How awesome is this place!'[1] For Jacob, the ladder was fixed, not moveable; and he named the place Bethel, the house of God.

Yet 'true worshippers will worship the father in spirit and in truth'[2]; and not exclusively in one place, for

Where can I go from your Spirit?	If I rise on the wings of the dawn,
where can I flee from your presence?	if I settle on the far side of the sea,
If I go up to the heavens, you are there;	Even there your hand will guide me,
if I make my bed in the depths, you are there.	your right hand will hold me fast.[3]

---

[1] Gen 28:12-17
[2] John 4:23
[3] Ps 139:7-10

So a nomadic narrowboat named *Jacob's Ladder* emphasised that the link between earth and heaven is everywhere, and in a chilly bare winter valley, with limp straw-coloured rushes fringing an icy canal, and the occasional wren flickering in and out of the brown hedgerows, and the North wind encouraging a very brisk pace, I could still think 'how awesome is this place!'

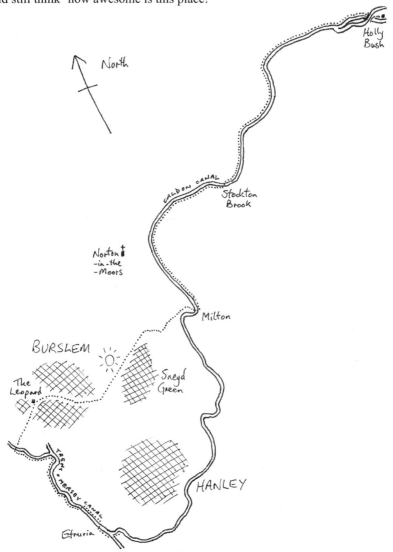

Map for chapters 9 & 10

In 1775 Josiah Wedgwood the one-legged potter rode this way, inspecting the route of the canal, surveyed but not yet built. For all his natural optimism, Wedgwood may have had solemn thoughts as he rode, for three years earlier his friend Brindley had surveyed the route, and in the process had been soaked through and caught a chill. On top of diabetes and chronic overwork and exhaustion, this finished him off. He was only 56, and had been married just seven years. Wedgwood for one was conscious that it was a great loss, writing to another friend, Thomas Bentley:

> He has left two young Children behind him, and poor Mrs Brindley, inconsolable for the loss of a sensible friend and affectionate Husband. What the public has lost can only be conceived by those who best knew his Character and Talents, Talents to which this Age and Country are indebted for works that will be the most lasting Monuments to his Fame, and shew to future Ages how much good may be done by one single Genius, when happily employed upon works beneficial to Mankind.

Did Brindley's death, showing the dangers of overwork, make Wedgwood consider his own workrate? He had been warning Brindley to ease off for years, yet he kept up a relentless schedule himself. Perhaps he told himself to delegate more, and reassured himself that his responsibilities were not so geographically divided as his late friend's had been. Nevertheless he did catch a cold himself, which his daughter Sukey teasingly referred to as 'a navigation cold'; so perhaps it was not the first time he had come home with a cold after riding to view canal construction or survey work.

The Caldon Canal was certainly a lasting monument to Brindley's expertise: it was highly successful, carrying commercial traffic for over 170 years. For a long time it was owned by the North Staffordshire Railway, which, being a local concern, had a good idea of its usefulness, saw it as a complementary business rather than part of the competition, and kept it in reasonable order. Once the NSR was absorbed into the LMSR group in 1923, the Caldon Canal was soon forgotten and neglected, and had to go through a period of near-disuse before its eventual restoration.

I was thankful for the restoration, as I walked the towpath. Although this was often deep in mud the colour of charcoal, the cold was sufficient to make the mud pretty firm, if not quite rock-hard. By a section that would have been exceedingly glutinous in warm wet weather, I was startled by several ostrich heads peering over the hedge. They didn't seem quite like pets, so were presumably being raised for the innovative restaurant trade, though it didn't sound very Staffordshire. Ostrich and mushroom oatcake, anyone? In a neighbouring pen were some llamas, or maybe they were alpacas, farmed for wool rather than meat. My father tells me that one beast will guard a flock of sheep against dogs, or be company for an aged pet pony.

Near Endon a man in orange gear was cutting hedges, and a string of boats were moored; none of the names was particularly unusual, but the combination suggested relaxation and love – of nature or of individuals: *Eventide, Barnaby, Sunseeker, Breeze, Misty Morn II,* and *Louisa.*.

Coming towards Stockton Brook, I met the first moving boat of the day: *Mandarin* was chugging along accompanied by sounds of crunching and cracking as the thin film of ice gave way to her steel bows. Further down Stockton Brook Locks, I saw that *Mandarin* couldn't have come far that morning, since the ice was undisturbed from bank to bank.

According to an old diary, I'd been here before, on another of Chris Parker's one-week barge trips: on 12th April 1985, we'd moored up and spent the night at Stockton Brook. As I walked down the locks twenty years later, nothing was familiar, but on that barge trip I'd caught a chill myself, and spent most of the last two days of the holiday lying in a bunk feeling grotty – the result of an extended turn steering the boat while a north wind was flinging sleet at my back. Understandably none of the rest of the crew had been especially keen to take over the helm until the sleet stopped. Still, unlike Brindley, I was young, not overworked, and generally healthy, so had recovered by the third day. But I didn't see much of the Caldon Canal that year.

All the more reason to appreciate it now. A kestrel swooped by on russet wings, and swept up to perch on the branch of a gaunt oak tree. Approaching Engine Lock, the skyline showed signs that a town was nearby: brick houses lined the brow of the hill, and beside them a dark red brick church crouched low, its squat tower hardly showing above the roofs. A sign by the lock identified the church, advertising 'St Bartholomew's Church, Norton-le-Moors, services 10.00 and 6.30'. Nearby were

 some large grey cattle with long down- and inward-pointing horns: English Longhorns. Before long the canal was curving round Milton, and a series of back gardens were making the most of their canal frontage, with terraces, benches, and appropriate ornaments. In one place a substantial slipway slanted up to someone's patio. On the slipway was parked the narrowboat *Treble Joy*; and in the canal below floated *Hedgehog*.

A floating hedgehog naturally called Kipling's *Just So Stories* to mind:

"Hold up my chin, Slow-and-Solid. I'm going to try to learn to swim. It may be useful."
"Excellent!" said Slow-and-Solid, and he held up Stickly-Prickly's chin, while Stickly-Prickly kicked in the waters of the turbid Amazon.

Beyond Milton Bridge the towpath looked as though it was blocked by construction work, and since I was aiming to turn off soon and strike across the urban landscape to Burslem, this seemed a good place to take to the streets. At first they were very nondescript: a few suburban roads, then workshops and light industry; but unexpectedly a path led away under trees and a brown sign proclaimed Holden Pools Nature Reserve. The path led roughly in the right direction, and a nature reserve had to be better than the streets, but if there was no way out at the other end it would mean a lot of extra walking, and I was beginning to think quite hard about lunch.

It was worth a small risk, I decided, heading into what seemed at first more of a Litter Reserve than anything to do with nature. The ground under the trees to the left was so thickly decorated with cans, bottles, paper and plastic that you would imagine teams of volunteers had been needed to supply it all; perhaps it was an avant-garde work of art, an 'installation', an ironic comment on urban life. Approaching the Pool itself, however, litter levels fell to the barely noticeable, and the birdlife on the water became the focus of attention: gulls, mallard, coots, a great crested grebe and a lot of tufted duck.

The last are always fun to watch; the drakes look smart with their black coats and white flanks, but most appealing is the sudden alacrity with which they dive and vanish, to pop up again cheerfully, somewhere quite different. They are delightful birds, and apparently also delicious; Bewick quotes Latham on foreign gastrono-my: 'the French allow these birds to be eaten on maigre days and in lent; as they do also the Scoter: but though the flesh of the latter is now and then tolerable, that of the Tufted Duck is seldom otherwise than excellent'.[1]

Tufted Duck do well on man-made water, which is usually deeper than natural small lakes and ponds. They dive quite deep, liking water around ten or fifteen feet in depth, and feeding on molluscs and shrimps near or on the bottom; they are less vegetarian than many ducks. They were once only winter visitors to England; but they seem to like the country and are breeding and staying in increasing numbers. Since they can find all they need in one place they are seen on the wing rather less than mallard.[2]

There was, of course, a way out at the other end of the reserve, and soon I was on the Leek New Road with not much more than a mile to go. On the map it looked as though part of the way could be through parkland; but close up the park turned out to be a very steep hill which was presumably a reclaimed slagheap. I wondered whether I could find the energy for a stiff climb, decided I ought to, but then on approaching the slope came to a lot of standing water. I returned to the road, consoling myself that the road was actually the shorter route.

Round a corner I finally saw Burslem, from this distance just a jumble of small buildings covering a hill. J.B. Priestley, coming to the Potteries in the 1930s, remarked on the 'littleness' of a 'Lilliputian' townscape where everything was 'stunted in height' and nothing caused the pedestrian to stare upward.[3]

A little way down the hill to the right, though not really visible from where I was, would be the home of Port Vale FC, one of the honest humble clubs that make up the numbers in the football league. Port Vale were never in the top division, never won a major trophy, and generally had little ambition beyond beating local rivals Stoke City and Crewe Alexandra, or gaining promotion if they happened to be in an even

[1] Bewick, *op cit*
[2] Gooders, J & Boyer, T (1986) *Ducks of Britain* Dragon's World
[3] Priestley, *op cit*

humbler league than usual. They survived, through most of their long history from 1876, by developing young footballers and selling them at a profit.

The great exponent of this ability to stay solvent by spotting talent was the manager John Rudge, who stayed nearly two decades at the club, pulling off deals such as the signing of Robbie Earle for peanuts, eventually selling him for £775,000, then replacing him (after lurking in a non-league car park to get his man) with the £15,000 Ian Taylor, (left) who scored bucketfuls of goals for two seasons before being sold for a million.

But the team wasn't always successful, with the best players, such as the elusive winger Steve Guppy, forever moving on to balance the books. After many years of standing by their manager, making him the second longest-serving in the entire league, the directors suddenly changed tack and sacked him with barely a thankyou. The fans were so disgusted at this ungrateful behaviour that they staged a march in protest: hundreds of men and boys marching through Burslem, all wearing flat caps in tribute to Rudge's habitual headgear (left). Fifty years earlier that might have looked quite normal; but by the end of the millennium it was a singular enough sight for the Flat Cap March to pass into local folklore.

By now my stride had shortened somewhat, and muscles were stiffening, after striding out perhaps a little too vigorously in the cold six miles earlier. It was disturbing, therefore, to see out of the corner of my eye a notice sternly warning 'Kerb crawlers will be arrested'. As pure reflex, I speeded up a little. The notice carried a police logo, was headlined 'Operation Justice', and added ominously 'this is just the start'. Just the start! So when all the kerb crawlers are locked up, they'll come for the pavement plodders, the pathway potterers, the driveway dodderers, the highway hobblers and the byway bumblers, not to mention the towpath toddlers. How fast do you have to go to feel safe? The thought of where it might all end kept me going briskly into Nile Street, which Arnold Bennett, who liked to rename everything, but kept the names helpfully transparent, called Aboukir Street.

At a crossroads the road ran under what had once been a railway bridge, now demolished: the former track of the famous Loop Line would have run over it. This began as a branch from Etruria to Hanley; a proposal to extend this through Cobridge, Burslem and Tunstall to rejoin the main line at Kidsgrove was welcomed locally, until the capital cost gave the North Staffordshire Railway cold feet. The NSR wanted to shelve the whole idea, but once the public had got hold of it, they would not let go, and the railway company had to abandon abandonment (how abandoned can you get?) and build the line.

The locals loved their Loop; it was convenient, cheap, regular and practical, with little North Staffordshire tank engines and short four-coach trains bustling to and fro with frequent stops at stations mostly a mile or less apart. It ran through picturesque industrial scenes: steelworks, brickworks and mills; past bottle kilns and coal mines and colliers' backyards.

Here between Cobridge and Burslem a local writer mentions a branch to Sneyd Colliery, a siding for tile factories, 'stacks of drainage pipes and gutters', and 'a large marlhole half-filled with water'.[1] It was an early version of urban rapid transit that would cost untold millions to build today. However, after the second World War it was less well supported, and so it was listed by the dreaded Dr. Beeching and closed in 1964. Now part of it has been converted into a cycleway as part of the 'greening' of the Potteries.

From here, if there had been more time and lunch had seemed less of a priority, I could have made a very short detour to see the Moorcroft factory, with its richly coloured and brilliantly glazed collectables. But the need to press on prevailed, and I kept going towards the centre of Burslem, the Mother Town of the Potteries. Once it had been little more than a village; at Domesday there was land in 'Barcadeslim' for two ploughs.

Gradually Burslem developed a cottage industry of crude earthenware pottery. But in 1647 plague arrived and devastated the small community, particularly the unsavoury Holehouse and Hot Lane districts. The many dead were piled in great pits away from the churchyard, and 'so great was the distress that an order was made for a special tax to assist the bereaved'.[2] Eventually the town recovered, and Wedgwood and others restored its reputation as the preeminent pottery town (at least, in its own opinion), although a few primitive practices persisted, such as throwing staves at a tethered cockerel.

As a justification for this activity, it was claimed that the local Saxons had been in conflict with some Danes, and had planned to attack at cock-crow. The wretched bird either crowed at the wrong time, or failed to crow at all; at any rate, the subsequent defeat was blamed on the cockerel, and a spiteful revenge had been enacted annually thereafter. More probably the tale was concocted as a convenient excuse for some popular cruelty.

---

[1] Brailsford, D (1978) *Reminiscences of the Knotty*
[2] Warrillow, EJD (1960) *A Sociological History of Stoke-on-Trent* Etruscan Publications

Ten: Burslem to Etruria *(2 miles)*

Big James – the Budgeon – Childgrove – clogs and rounded calves – clog tunes – quizzical arch – four famous men – Black Bull – disaster of disasters – roast mutton – jolly bizarre – runaway pantechnicon

24th January 2005

Before long I was passing the Royal Doulton works and climbing the last short hill to the George Hotel, which Arnold Bennett renamed the Dragon (it had once been the George & Dragon). I had thought I might look for lunch there, to have a look at the interior, which features in his novels of the Five Towns, but the George's menu seemed altogether too grand for me.

In *Clayhanger* Bennett gives us a rare picture of popular music in the assembly room of the Dragon in Bursley (Burslem) in the year 1872: concertina-playing, handbell-ringing, and a 'performance on the ophicleide, a serpentine instrument that coiled round and about its player, and when breathed into persuasively gave forth prodigious brassy sounds that resembled the night-noises of beasts of prey.' And then...

'Gentlemen all, Mr James Yarlett will now kindly oblige with *The Miller of the Dee.*'

...Big James's rendering of *The Miller of the Dee* had been renowned in the Five Towns since 1852. It was classical, hallowed. It was the only possible rendering of *The Miller of the Dee.* If the greatest bass in the world had come incognito to Bursley and sung *The Miller of the Dee*, people would have said, 'Ah! But ye should hear Big James sing it!' It suited Big James. The sentiments of the song were his sentiments; he expressed them with natural simplicity; but at the same time they underwent a certain refinement at his hands; for even when he sang at his loudest Big James was refined, natty, and restrained... And the real beauty and enormous power of his magnificent voice saved him by its mere distinction from the charge of being finicking. The simple sound of the voice gave pleasure. And the simple production of that sound was Big James's deepest joy...

A version of the *Miller of the Dee* was discovered in 1857 on the fly-leaf of a volume of Dryden's poetry printed in 1716. The following verse is distinctly more sententious than other versions of the song, and the sturdy Victorian work ethic expressed may well represent Big James's own sentiments:

The reason why he was so blithe he once did thus unfold,
'The bread I eat my hands have earned; I covet no man's gold;
I do not fear next quarterday; in debt to none I be,
I care for nobody no, not I, if nobody cares for me.'

The melody now associated with *The Miller of the Dee*, the tune Big James surely sang, could be found earlier as the tune to *The Budgeon it is a Delicate Trade*, a delightfully obscure canting song in the 1728 Quakers' Opera (*budgeon* is pickpocketing, and the *cully* is the victim):

The budgeon it is a delicate trade, and a delicate trade of fame,
For when that we have bit the bloe, we carry away the game.
But if the cully nab us, and the lurries from us take,
Oh then he rubs us to the whit, though we are not worth a make.

And earlier still, the 1650 Playford dance tune *Childgrove* is clearly the parent
of the Budgeon tune, though the latter has been sweetened and sentimentalised from
the astringent simplicity of the earlier melody.

Back at the Dragon, Big James's performance is by no means the final one of
the evening. A recitation follows, and then:

'Gentlemen all, Miss Florence Simcox – or shall us say Mrs Offlow, wife
of the gentleman who has just obliged – the champion female clog-dancer of the
Midlands, will now oblige.'

...when Florence shone suddenly at the service-door, the shortness of her
red-and-black velvet skirts, and the undeniable complete visibility of her rounded calves produced an uneasy and agreeable impression...the smile between
[her] shaking golden ringlets had neither the modesty nor the false modesty nor
the docility that Bursley was accustomed to think proper to the face of woman.
It could have stared down any man in the place...

She danced; and the service-doorway showed a vista of open-mouthed
scullions. There was no sound in the room, save the concertina and the champion clogs. Every eye was fixed on those clogs...Florence herself chiefly gazed
on those clogs...at intervals, with her ringed fingers she would lift the short skirt
- a nothing, an imperceptibility, half an inch, with glance downcast; and the
effect was profound, recondite, inexplicable. Her style was not that of a male
clog-dancer, but it was indubitably clog-dancing, full of marvels to the connois-
seur, and to the profane naught but a highly complicated series of wooden
noises...The clog, the very emblem of the servitude and the squalor of brutalized
populations, was changed, on the light feet of this favourite, into the medium of
grace. Few of these men but at some time in their lives had worn the clog, had
clattered in it through winter's slush, and through the freezing darkness before
dawn, to the manufactory and the mill and the mine, whence after a day of labour

under discipline more than military, they had clattered back to their little candle-lighted homes…the clog meant everything that was harsh, foul, and desolating; it summoned images of misery and disgust. Yet on those feet that had never worn it seriously, it became the magic instrument of pleasure, waking dulled wits and forgotten aspirations, putting upon everybody an enchantment…

What images does the clog summon today? For many, perhaps none at all: some might not even be sure what a clog looks like. For others, the idea of a clog – hand-made and expensive – might carry connotations of environmental soundness, quaintness, alternative lifestyles, vegetarianism, ethnic clothing acquired in craft fairs or charity shops…anything but a working-class item, the 21st century clog. To enter the experience Bennett describes needs a considerable leap of imagination. At least clog-dancing can still be seen and appreciated; and concertinas are still played. I would have liked some idea of the melody the concertina was playing…did Bennett actually have music running through his head as he pictured the scene, or was his imagination purely visual, verbal, and philosophical?

The following two tunes have been edited slightly, changing a few unimportant notes to make them easier to play on the whistle, and changing the key of each so that the two can be played consecutively on the same (E flat) whistle.

The Fancy Clog

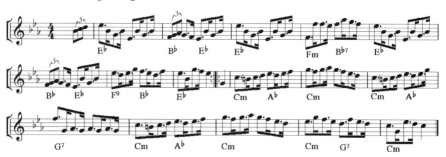

The Champion Clog

90

The popular musical traditions in the Potteries did not remain confined to the local pub. Although many working folk had problems learning to read staff music, once Josiah Powell, the Burslem Registrar, had decided to try tonic sol-fa, the idea quickly caught on, amateur choirs improved rapidly, and they frequently did well in regional and even national competition. In 1884 the Burslem Tonic Sol-fa Choir took first prize at the Welsh National Eisteddfod, beating their Potteries rivals the Hanley Glee and Madrigal Society into second place.

Remembering Bennett's descriptions as I stood outside the George (or Dragon), I reluctantly decided to go somewhere humbler for lunch, and headed off across Swan Square. Up to my right was the Town Hall, where in 1861 hundreds of disappointed folk were milling about outside, having failed to get into the packed auditorium. Richard Weaver, the 'Converted Collier', was preaching on behalf of the Ragged Schools, a cause that Burslem folk embraced with fervent energy.

I walked down Queen Street, past the grand School of Art and the splendid Burslem Library with its ornate statues. The School of Art was opened in 1863 with immense pomp, a fanfare of trumpets, and a very long speech by W.E. Gladstone, then Chancellor of the Exchequer. To lay the foundation stone the great man was supplied with an ornate china trowel embellished with gold, silver, and heraldic medallions.

The School of Art naturally focused on the practical application of artistic talent within the needs of the local industry, hoping to bring new insights to the form and embellishment of pottery. One of the best known alumni was Susie Cooper, a designer of elegance and originality, whose own pose in the classic old photograph shows just those qualities: the perfect angle of the hat, the cool and quizzical arch of the eyebrows, the detached appraising gaze.

Beyond the School of Art I turned right into Brick House St and walked up to the Market Place. There I found the Leopard (which Bennett calls the Tiger), a historic Burslem pub complete with densely patterned upholstery, leaded stained glass, polished wood, china plates on racks near the ceiling, and a middle-aged woman complaining bitterly about the misfortunes of Port Vale Football Club.

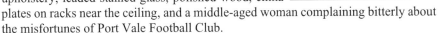

Much of the ambience (apart from the last in the list) might already have been present in March 1765, when four famous men met in the Leopard to discuss a possible canal project. It was the first time Josiah Wedgwood the potter, Thomas Bentley the merchant, Erasmus Darwin the doctor, and James Brindley the millwright had all four come together; and the project would eventually become the Trent & Mersey Canal, which now passes about a mile from the scene of this historic meeting.

Wedgwood was the host, still two-legged at this date; the Leopard was his local, just round the corner from the Bell Works, where his premises were at that time (Etruria still lay in the future). He knew each of the other three men, but they had not all met each other. He seems to have had a leaning to strong friendships; he and Bentley took to each other at their first meeting in Liverpool, while he shared much with Darwin on the scientific-intellectual level. In Brindley he admired industry and perfectionism. Perhaps before this meeting he was as hopeful that his three friends would like each other, as that the project would get under way.

Bentley   *Wedgwood*   *Darwin*   *Brindley*

It was not particularly surprising that they did, though later Darwin and Bentley sometimes clashed. The men were from a roughly similar level of society: families prosperous enough to own businesses and give their sons an education, but not so elevated as to disdain hard work, trade, or learning. Brindley was the senior man, at forty-nine years of age; the other three were thirty-four or five. All of them were in one way or another idealists and visionaries, ready to improve the lot of man and believing, in the spirit of the Age of Enlightenment, that it was eminently possible to do so. Putting together Bentley's persuasive salesmanship, Darwin's enthusiasm, Wedgwood's persistence, and Brindley's expertise in harnessing water, it would have been difficult to assemble four men better qualified to realize the vision of a waterway linking the Midlands with the North Sea, Bristol, Liverpool, and ultimately London.

Happy to be in such distinguished company (including both of Charles Darwin's grandfathers), I invested in some egg mayonnaise sandwiches and Theakston's Black Bull bitter, to provide fuel for the walk down to and along the Trent & Mersey. Theakston's had once been a celebrated independent brewery, but now it was part of Scottish & Newcastle, whose distribution network explained why this Yorkshire beer was to be found in Staffordshire. Black Bull, according to CAMRA, has 'a distinctively hoppy aroma', which 'leads to a bitter, hoppy taste with some fruitiness and a short bitter finish. Rather thin', they add disapprovingly; but I didn't find it so.

After lunch, it was time to head for the Trent & Mersey, hoping to trace (in reverse) the steps of Arnold Bennett's character Edwin Clayhanger, walking home to Burslem from his school in Newcastle. More than a century earlier, the young Josiah Wedgwood would have walked, or maybe run, the same way.

This route took me through the sloping St John's Square, which in the early nineteenth century had been the place to take a horse-drawn coach if you wanted to travel to other towns. The 'Potter' would convey you to Manchester; the 'Red Rover' to London or Liverpool; and the 'Hark Forward' to Birmingham. Most towns of any size had had coaches passing through for a hundred years or so, but the roads in the Potteries were so rough and muddy that for a long time the private coach companies avoided them. The elite coach, the Royal Mail, never did venture directly into the Potteries before the coming of the railways. This irritated the local businessmen for several reasons: they got their post late, they had to pay extra for it, and the private coaches were much less secure, lacking the armed guards of the Royal Mail, and thus encouraging criminal attack. The 'Potter' was once robbed of £5000 which was in transit to a bank branch. Impassioned pleas for a proper postal service fell on deaf ears:

> Why are our pockets thus constantly to suffer? Are we without claim to what is considered a general convenience? Have not the Staffordshire Potteries, a district of twelve miles, and containing sixty thousand inhabitants, equal claim with Newcastle, Stone, and others, for a regular Mail? ... Countrymen, let us boldly show to all that we are Britons; that we are sensible of having a common right to a common convenience; and let us respectfully, yet confidently, represent our inconveniences to the Honourable His Majesty's Post-Master-General, and claim the redress we so fully need...[1]

Halfway down Furlong Lane, I saw the first brick bottle kilns since I'd walked into the Potteries; once they were everywhere, you couldn't not see them. Now just a few remain to keep the Six Towns distinctive. Pottery became a local trade because of the simultaneous availability of coal, ironstone, clay, and water.

The precariousness of the pottery trade, and the skills involved, are caught by another local novelist, John Wain, in a racy description by one of his characters:

> In the pottery industry, a spoilt kiln is the disaster of disasters. When the ware is ready for firing, they stack it in the kiln (pronounced 'kill' locally, for some reason), and keep it at a fantastic temperature for about thirty hours. This temperature has to be even and the art of firing is to feed the coal in so that it doesn't vary; if it wanders up and down, the entire contents of the 'kill' come out distorted and have to be thrown away. And that means several hundred pounds' worth of pottery.[2]

For a small business, that could mean bankruptcy; so small firms were starting up or going under all the time, and a factory might change hands quite often. And thus a successful manufacturer like Josiah Wedgwood could move to larger premises and yet larger before investing in building his own.

Between some old mills that looked almost derelict ran an alley that led to a canal bridge. It might have been the site of Clayhanger's meeting with Charlie Orgreave, where they watch two barges approaching, one bringing china clay from

[1] cited in Warrillow, 1960, *op cit*

[2] Wain, J (1958) *The Contenders* Macmillan

...like giant Burgundy bottles...

Cornwall, the other taking pottery to Liverpool, and bet on which will reach the bridge first. Even if it was the right place, however, it wasn't the same bridge, but a twentieth-century replacement.

Just round the corner from here, at Brownhills, was where work was begun on the Trent & Mersey, or the Grand Trunk Canal, as it was originally called. 26th July, 1766 was a holiday for the workers of Burslem, and they turned out for the speeches and celebrations, and to watch Josiah Wedgwood dig the first spadeful of earth, and dump it in a barrow for James Brindley to trundle away. Grand and celebrated men they doubtless were, but they were also men of their hands, who probably made such ceremony look more natural than Gladstone might have done with his fancy trowel. The ceremony completed, provision for the populace was generous:

> ...a barrel of old Staffordshire ale was broached on the spot... Succeeding to this were luncheons and dinners at the Leopard and other inns... A sheep was roasted whole for the benefit of the poorer potters, and at sunset bonfires were lighted in various parts of the town.[1]

Ishbel and I saw whole sheep roasting on spits quite often, during our year in Bosnia; so we could not just see the scene in our minds' eyes, but smell it in our minds' noses: roast mutton with a background of woodsmoke and ale. Back in English Middleport, the scene was very quiet and peaceful, almost deserted. There was no sign as yet of any action on the £3million plans to redevelop Middleport using the canal as a feature:

> The Middleport Waterfront Town Heritage Initiative will see the restoration of landmark buildings and the regeneration of derelict land that surrounds the Trent and Mersey Canal, one of the busiest stretches of waterway in the country.[2]

Middleport was not that busy in January: there were no barges moving as I set off southwards on a firm towpath that was embellished at intervals with abstract steel structures carrying informative plaques. The canal was at least usable and cared for; in its heyday it had been owned by the North Staffordshire Railway, who invested in their own canal to support it in its rivalry with the Shropshire Union, which was owned by the LNWR.

Yet in the 1950s and 60s it became a matter for discussion whether there would be any 'pleasure boats' using the stretch of the Trent & Mersey through the Potteries, and therefore whether it was worth the expense of maintaining this length.[3] Harecastle tunnel was not cheap, and some would not have worried at the thought of severing the link between the Macclesfield and Caldon canals. There would still have been a north-south link, they might have argued, via the Shropshire Union. The commercial traffic that was still serving the local industries was not sufficient to pay for the upkeep of the canal, and should be transferred to the roads.

[1] Meteyard, E (1866) *Life of Josiah Wedgwood,* cited in *Hadfield's British Canals*
[2] *The Sentinel,* a local newspaper cited in *Waterways,* Feb 2005
[3] Suleman, *op cit*

The extent of official disdain for the narrow canals is hard to imagine today, but the following pronouncement from the British Transport Commission gives a flavour of what the first canal enthusiasts had to contend with:

> These uneconomic canals are no longer required for transport purposes, and the chief need is for greater expedition in the proceedings involved in formal abandonment and in transfer, where appropriate, to other authorities interested in them for various purposes (e.g. land drainage).[1]

It took decades of stubborn fighting by pioneers such as Robert Aickman to convince the authorities of the potential amenity value of the canals, and the importance of keeping as much as possible navigable, rather than abandoning as much as possible. Now the Trent & Mersey through the Potteries and Harecastle Tunnel is a vital link which is used by a lot of pleasure boats from spring to autumn, though relatively little in winter.

Tom Chaplin, a former boatman in the last days of commercial freight, laments the barrenness of the canals in winter nowadays, with nothing moving: no icebreakers, no well-muffled boatpeople battling the cold and gaining the satisfaction of getting their cargo through against the odds; no snug little cabin whose cosiness was most enhanced by bleak conditions outside; no bold bright colours of traditional narrow-boat decoration to contrast with the muted misty shades of a winter day.[2]

Here in Middleport was once the boatyard of the Anderton Company, canal carriers on a large scale, mainly between the Potteries and the River Weaver. They were famous for the 'knobstick' artwork of Bill Hodgson, who painted the traditional roses and castles throughout the first half of the last century. He used a more naturalistic style than many others, especially in his roses. Why they were known as 'knobstick' is hard to tell now, but it has been suggested that that was originally the nickname of the company, rather than just the painting style, which poses the further question of why the company had that nickname. The Anderton Company went back to 1836, but existed as Alexander Reid & Co even before that, so the nickname could be a very old one.

Soon I came to the site of the vanished Burslem Arm (which should soon reappear as part of the regeneration scheme); somewhere near here was once the Newport Pottery, where Clarice Cliff (left) worked between the two world wars. Here she produced the 'Bizarre' range of Art Deco pottery, aimed at the cheap Woolworth's market, but nowadays highly popular among collectors.

---

[1] cited in Bolton, D (1990) *Race Against Time* Methuen
[2] Chaplin, T (2ed 1989) *Narrow Boats* Whittet

Clarice Cliff was almost exactly contemporary with Susie Cooper, but very different in personality, style, and career; and her creations were as different as could be within the fashions of the twenties and thirties. She had left school at thirteen, starting as an enameller at a pottery, and only fitted in formal study of art later. In contrast to Cooper's cool and stylish appearance, and the sophisticated grace of her designs, Cliff was cheerful and jolly, and her crockery was original in form, and jazzily bold in colour and decoration: less beautiful, but more memorable.

The Burslem Arm would also have been one of the locations where Bennett's *The Card* was filmed (starring Alec Guinness); somewhere nearby was the site of Denry's plunge into the canal, on board a runaway removal van that he was vainly attempting to stop. On the van's arrival in the water there is a surprise:

> ...the pantechnicon ... jolted over the iron guard of the weighing-machine, and this jolt deflected it, so that instead of aiming at the gates it aimed for part of a gate and part of a brick pillar. Denry ground his teeth together and clung to his seat. The gate might have been paper, and the brick pillar a cardboard pillar. The pantechnicon went through them as a sword will go through a ghost, and Denry was still alive. The remainder of the journey was brief and violent, owing partly to a number of bags of cement, and partly to the propinquity of the canal basin. The pantechnicon jumped into the canal like a mastodon, and drank.
>
> Denry, clinging to the woodwork, was submerged for a moment, but, by standing on the narrow platform from which sprouted the splintered ends of the shafts, he could get his waist clear of the water. He was not a swimmer.
>
> All was still and dark, save for the faint stream of starlight on the broad bosom of the canal basin. The pantechnicon had encountered nobody whatever *en route*. Of its strange escapade Denry had been the sole witness.
>
> 'Well, I'm dashed!' he murmured aloud.
>
> And a voice replied from the belly of the pantechnicon:
>
> 'Who is there?'[1]

The story is well worth reading; I won't give the continuation away. As I walked along the grey canal in the cold January light, the darkness of the scene of Denry's adventure took a little effort of imagination. Beyond the site of the old Burslem Arm were two more well-preserved bottle kilns, whose restorers advertised themselves with a large billboard: 'Olivers Mill: consolidation works and conservation repairs to two Grade II listed late 19th century calcining kilns'. Calcining was baking flints so that they would become brittle and easy to grind up. So here the kilns were right by the canal, to enable the flints to be transferred direct from the narrow-boats – maybe John Walley's, a carrier that specialised in flint, with smart boats painted in all the primary colours: black, white, red, green, blue and yellow.

After the next bridge the surroundings opened out into a wide flat post-demolition desert, where nothing was standing except one tall brick chimney in empty space, and some way beyond it, a single immense length of factory wall in blackened steel.

---

[1] Bennett, A (1911) *The Card*

Eleven: Etruria to Hanley *(1½ miles)*

*Rivers of fire – unwanted smoke – forgotten mackerel – throwing black basalt –
doubtful virgin – Gossip Joan – Bread Riots – turmoil of flames – icy gasometers –
Lamplighter's Hornpipe – blue hands – the nearest place to the bottomless pit – black
snow – revival – introspection in the Five Towns*

24th *January 2005*

I was passing the site of Shelton Bar Ironworks, which was founded by Lord
Granville in 1839, when he leased the land from the Duchy of Lancaster. Four
hundred and fifty feet below ground were the strata of black band ironstone; and there
was also coal close by. The company prospered through the Victorian era and into the
twentieth century; at their centenary they employed six thousand miners and three
thousand steelworkers. It was an unmissable local landmark, and the fictional Edwin
Clayhanger and his friend gazed intently from a distance as the ironworks discharged
molten slag:

> To the south of them, a mile and a half off, in the wreathing mist of the
> Cauldon Bar Ironworks, there was a yellow gleam that even the capricious sunlight
> could not kill, and then two rivers of fire sprang from the gleam and ran in a
> thousand delicate and lovely hues down the side of a mountain of refuse. They
> were emptying a few tons of molten slag at the Cauldon Bar Ironworks. The two
> rivers hung slowly dying in the mists of smoke. They reddened and faded, and you
> thought they had vanished, and you could see them yet, and then they escaped the
> baffled eye, unless a cloud aided them for a moment against the sun; and their
> ephemeral but enchanting beauty had expired for ever.[1]

Now there was nothing visible from where I was walking to show the exact site
of the long-vanished ironworks; a high bank on the far side of the canal might have
been reclaimed slag, but now it was well-grassed and overgrown. A fox appeared at
the top of the bank and gazed down at me with frank interest, head cocked a little
sideways; then turned and disappeared through a fence. A little further on the towpath
crossed over to the east bank, and the west bank was taken over by some very
new-looking office buildings with a neat canal frontage.

Two employees were smoking outside; at least these banished smokers had a
pleasant canal view, and the company had thoughtfully provided a tiny shelter for
rainy days, though it couldn't have kept the rain off more than three smokers at once.
These were changed days for the Potteries, where cigarette smoke used to seem less
toxic than the surrounding atmosphere; now the wisp of sidestream smoke from a
single fag was unwanted.

Round another bend was the Black Prince Marina, a sizeable basin filled with
innumerable narrowboats, on the site where the canal was widened between Etruria
Hall, the Wedgwood residence, and their pottery works. Wedgwood had wanted a
graceful curve to the canal, to give a picturesque view from the Hall, but Brindley
jibbed at the idea of an unnecessary bend.

[1] Bennett, A (1910) *Clayhanger*

Although many of his canals wound and meandered, that was forced by the contours; he wanted a straight line when he could get one. The compromise was to widen the canal and include a small island with trees and bushes, which can be seen in old engravings of the scene.

The island sank long ago due to mining subsidence, but was much loved while it existed. In the days before bathing costumes became universal, one vicar of Etruria used to swim to the island and sunbathe there; and more than once a mischievous parishioner removed the vicar's clothes and attached them to the Vicarage doorknob, leaving the vicar to run home nude across the fields. The Reverend Topham was said to have been a jolly and confident chap who probably took the joke in good part. He was also unselfconscious enough to turn up for a service once with 'a large mackerel sticking out of his hip pocket – a purchase made on the Saturday night in the fish market, and one which he had forgotten to remove.'[1]

At the next bridge the towpath switched sides again, passing the Rotunda, a brick structure as round as its name suggested, and the only remaining part of Wedgwood's Etruria Works. A plaque informed the curious and ignorant that once the Rotunda had stood at towpath level, which was difficult to imagine, as now half its substantial height was below the canal. This serious subsidence, combined with a lack of room for expansion, persuaded the Wedgwood company to move their production to a new greenfield site in the middle of the twentieth century, after 181 years at Etruria. I would eventually see the new factory as I walked south on the Trent & Mersey.

Just under three years after the jollifications to mark the beginning of work on the Grand Trunk Canal, Josiah Wedgwood had another excuse for a celebration: the opening of Etruria Works on June 13th, 1769. Once again he was prepared to roll his sleeves up and do something symbolic, yet practical, to mark the occasion:

> Mr. Wedgwood removed his hat and coat and tied on one of the white aprons used by his workmen, while an old servant prepared the balls of clay. Seated at the thrower's boards, whilst Mr. Bentley turned the wheel, he threw with great precision, and with the skill of one who had mastered the art from the beginning, six vases in black basalt body, to the cheers and encouragement of his family and friends.[2]

As before, lunch was provided, followed by festivities in glorious summer weather until sunset, and thus the new manufactory was well and truly launched. The name of Etruria, it is said, was suggested by Erasmus Darwin, who gives ample reason for this choice in his poetry, and extensive explanatory footnotes:

[1] Warrillow, EJD (1952) *History of Etruria* Etruscan Publications
[2] Warrillow, 1952, *op cit*

Etruria! next beneath thy magic hands
Glides the quick wheel, the plaistic clay expands,
Nerved with fine touch, thy fingers (as it turns)
Mark the nice bounds of vases, ewers, and urns;
Round each fair form in lines immortal trace
Uncopied Beauty, and ideal Grace.

[*Note.* Etruria may perhaps vie with China itself in the antiquity of its arts. The times of its greatest splendour were prior to the foundations of Rome, and the reign of one of its best princes, Janus, was the oldest epoch the Romans knew. The earliest historians speak of the Etruscans as being then of high antiquity, most probably a colony from Phoenicia, to which a Pelasgian colony acceded, and was united soon after Deucalion's flood. The peculiar character of their earthen vases consists in the admirable beauty, simplicity, and diversity of forms, which continue the best models of taste to the artists of the present times; and in a species of non-vitreous encaustic painting, which was reckoned, even in the time of Pliny, among the lost arts of antiquity, but which has lately been recovered by the ingenuity and industry of Mr. Wedgwood. ... See D'Hancarville's preliminary discourses to the magnificent collection of Etruscan vases, published by Sir William Hamilton.]

Etruria Hall was built at the same time as the Works; Wedgwood was able to do this because of the money his wife Sarah had brought with her on their marriage. He consulted his Sally on all points of the site and design of the Hall, partly because he regarded the house as much, perhaps more, as hers than his; but equally because he simply valued her judgment, for he also continually consulted her on the designs of his products.

The Hall was a fine building with the simple quality and restrained ornamentation that were typical of Wedgwood's style. Here he could enjoy seclusion with his growing family, entertain friends such as Bentley or Darwin, and look out at his parkland stretching down to his factory beyond the canal that he had helped to promote. Here he could browse in his great library, that contained everything from the recently published *Tristram Shandy* to Hamilton's *Antiquities* ('My wife', he once wrote to a friend, 'says I must buy no more books till I build another house'). Here he could listen to Sukey, his favourite and firstborn, playing on the harpsichord, with her younger sister Kitty sometimes singing along.

Sukey was Susannah, who would later marry Erasmus Darwin's third son Robert, and become the mother of Charles Darwin. According to Jenny Uglow, Sukey was 'very like her father, outgoing, quick-thinking, stubborn;' he would 'always love her most among his many children'. [1]

Uglow quotes several extracts from Sukey's letters to her father, which give ample evidence of a complex and subtle sense of humour: droll, sardonic, gleeful or leg-pulling – a sense of humour which was shared and appreciated by Josiah. He was happy to indulge her interest in music, especially when she returned home after a serious illness, and lost patience with her first keyboard instrument:

[1] Uglow, J (2002) *The Lunar Men* Faber & Faber

Poor Sukey is quite out of patience with her old spinet & often asks me when her new one will come. I wrote to desire Mr Brock would acquaint Mr Williams that we had fix'd upon a double key'd instrument ... my girl is quite tired out with her present miserable hum strum...[1]

The miserable spinet was replaced by a harpsichord, which Wedgwood wanted Stubbs to include in the family portrait. He asked Stubbs to paint Sukey playing while Kitty sang; but Stubbs wanted outdoors and horses, and the painter carried his point.

What might Sukey (right) have played, for her sister Kitty to sing? 'A woman's work is never done', to the tune of the *Doubting Virgin*, was current in the eighteenth century, taken from one of the popular Ballad Operas. It might have appealed to Sukey's sense of irony, for although the sisters were born to wealth, and the Hall had a large staff of servants, their father's favourite eleventh commandment was 'Thou shalt not be idle': he kept them busy both in and out of the schoolroom. Sukey studied accounts, English, French, and 'fossiling' (ie geology in the field), as well as the traditionally ladylike pursuits of needlework and music.

> There's ne'er a day, from morn to night, but I with work am tired quite;
> For when the game is at the best, I hardly take one hour's rest;
> Sometimes I knit, and sometimes spin; sometimes I wash, and sometimes wring.
> Sometimes I sit, and sew alone, and a woman's work is never done.

But maybe something more cheerful would be called for, and *Good Morrow, Gossip Joan*, from an eighteenth century edition of *Pills to Purge Melancholy*, has the kind of strong melody that a little sister could easily master. One could imagine Sukey suggesting that Kitty sing 'vase' instead of 'glass', in the following verse, just to tease their father:

> My sparrow's flown away, and will no more come to me;
> I've broke a glass today, I've broke a glass today,
> The price will quite undo me, Gossip Joan

---

[1] Farrar, KE ed (1903) *Letters of Josiah Wedgwood*

Etruria Hall is now a smart four-star hotel, but it saw much neglect before its recent renovation. Later generations of Wedgwoods did not love it as Josiah had done, and the family moved out in the nineteenth century. By the mid-twentieth century it had been taken over by the Coal Board, and Professor Hoskins was shocked by its surroundings:

> Etruria Hall still stands, in a landscape of demonic ugliness, backed not by tiers of green woods but by colliery tips higher than itself, and in front, not an ornamental sheet of water but a filthy 'flash', dark with coal-dust, arising from subsidence due to coal-mining below.[1]

From the Hall to the Works was an easy walk, and in hard winters a direct route could be taken over the frozen canal; Francis Wedgwood, Josiah's grandson, made a habit of this. He got a shock one dark morning, for the ice-breaker had been through, yet a thin skin of ice had reformed, enough to look solid in dim light. Francis had 'an exciting few minutes' hauling himself out of the freezing water, but survived the experience.[2]

In 1783 Etruria was one of the flashpoints of the Bread Riots. At this time high food prices were causing distress among the poor, and some began to take matters into their own hands. Barges laden with flour and cheese, corn and barley, arrived at the wharf; but then the owners of the cargo ordered the bargemen to continue north to Manchester. The Etruria folk believed this was purely to get higher prices for the food, so took possession of the boats and sold off the cargoes at what they felt were fair prices, at first giving the proceeds to the barge captain. However some preferred to take more radical action; improvised weapons were stolen and a riot ensued that the militia eventually had to quell. It is said that Major Sneyd showed considerable patience, but finally ordered a charge and captured two ringleaders, employees at Wedgwood's. One was later hanged.

Although Wedgwood was much distressed by the whole situation, he had been unwilling to raise wages to a level where the high food prices would not be a problem. He was among the more generous and humane employers, but disliked the feeling that his good nature was being taken advantage of. After the riots he took the time to write a long pamphlet to his employees. His arguments, however, do not look compelling to modern eyes; one scholar calls them 'naïve', 'unconvincing' and even 'sheer hypocrisy'.[3]

Nevertheless Wedgwood was keen to improve the world in whatever way he could: he was active in the anti-slave trade movement, organising petitions, writing to friends and acquaintances to press the justice of the cause, and commissioning and producing the ceramic medallions of the kneeling chained slave that helped popularise the movement. Wilberforce came and stayed at Etruria Hall, and was impressed by both the house and the family, finding Sarah and the children 'sensible, spirited

---

[1] Hoskins, WG (1955) *The Making of the English Landscape* Hodder & Stoughton
[2] Warrillow, 1952, *op cit*
[3] Thomas, J (1971) *The Rise of the Staffordshire Potteries* Adams & Dart

[and] intelligent'.[1]

Not only have the Etruria Works of Wedgwood now disappeared, but also Etruria Grove, a famous long avenue of mature trees shading the road eastwards; and Etruria Woods on the hill above, where a profusion of bluebells soothed the convalescent H. G. Wells (right), visiting friends nearby. He used to rest in the woods, looking towards the Shelton Bar steelworks, and contemplating the differing beauties of the natural and industrial scenes. His short story 'The Cone' was conceived here, a gripping yarn – with a scorching conclusion – which includes descriptions that give a sharp delineation of the scene a hundred and more years ago:

> ...to the left... dominating the whole view, colossal, inky-black, and crowned with smoke and fitful flames, stood the great cylinders of the Jeddah Company Blast Furnaces, the central edifices of the big ironworks of which Horrocks was the manager. They stood heavy and threatening, full of an incessant turmoil of flames and seething molten iron, and about the feet of them rattled the rolling-mills, and the steam hammer beat heavily and splashed the white iron sparks hither and thither. Even as they looked, a truckful of fuel was shot into one of the giants, and red flames gleamed out, and a confusion of smoke and black dust came boiling upwards towards the sky.[2]

Nothing so dramatic was to be seen in the early 21st century, as I continued southwards on the towpath. Before long Etruria junction came into view. By the west bank of the canal here was once the Etruria Gas Works, 'one of the brightest jewels in the crown of the West Midlands Gas Board'.[3] Those of us old enough to remember working gasworks can still call up the memory of their reek in our nostrils, and might balk a little at calling them bright jewels. But an older generation still could remember when *everything* was coal-fired: every house, every foundry, every kiln. They knew how much less smoke and soot gas-firing involved; so for Warrillow, the historian of Etruria, its gasworks was 'this wonderful undertaking'. The fact that his father and grandfather were senior managers at the gasworks, and that he was born in the Gas Manager's house, may also have marginally influenced his positive impression. This inside knowledge included some dramatic stories: in another January, sixty-four years ago, there had been an air-raid:

> The whole of the Etruscan valley was covered in hard frost, with a little mist in the lower parts and lighted by a very brilliant moon, when the raiders flew in, following the railway line from Stoke. ...from Stoke, through Etruria towards Longport was one line of burning incendiaries, adding to the brilliance of the moonlit morning ... a number fell on each of the large gasholders... and great jets of flaming gas soared skywards from three of them.

[1] Reilly, R (1992) *Josiah Wedgwood* Macmillan
[2] Wells, HG (1895) 'The Cone' *Unicorn,* September 18, 1895
[3] Warrillow, 1952, *op cit*

Volunteers were called for and... the party bravely climbed the ladders of the giant holders. The crowns were covered in ice and reflected the moonlight like great mirrors. Walking on them was exceedingly dangerous, and a slip might well have meant death. The clay, which had been placed in readiness for just such an event, was frozen, adding to the difficulties... The enemy, seeing the blaze, returned to bomb the holders with high explosives. Fortunately, they were a little short of the target. The brave men continued their work under this intense attack, quite undefended, and completed it satisfactorily.[1]

If gasometers and gasworks are a thing of the past now, gaslight belongs to a yet more remote and romantic era. The image of the lamplighter, head tilted back and face illuminated by his own activity, as the long pole stretched to the tall lamp above, was a favourite one even when it was seen daily; now, distance lends enchantment: 'the elfin-like torch, with its tiny but bright light bobbing up and down at twilight' sticks in Warrillow's memory.

Lamplighter's Hornpipe

At the junction you had to cross the gate of the Top Lock on the Trent & Mersey, then the gate of the dry dock, to get to the towpath of the Caldon Canal. Here at the bottom of the Caldon was moored a handsome narrowboat: *White Quartz*, owned by Reg and Beryl, who had the good fortune to live here as well: beyond the boat was a well-tended garden, in which sat two flowerpot people, labeled 'Reg' and 'Bez', happily smiling and waving blue hands to passing cruisers and ramblers.

As I admired narrowboat, garden, and flowerpot sculpture, I was surprised by a friendly little border terrier bouncing up at my thigh. 'Get down, Molly!' commanded her owner; but you couldn't be offended by such friendliness. Some dogs jump up aggressively; some a bit over-exuberantly, but this was just good-natured cheerfulness.

---

[1] Warrillow, 1952, *op cit*

Further on, to the right, was an interesting-looking museum; no time to visit today, but I could come back with Ishbel. To the left was a landscaped area of former wharfage, featuring a statue of Brindley in grey stone, though pigeons and gulls had left him white-haired and white-shouldered. Round the first bend in the Caldon Canal was a strip of parkland between the staircase locks and some very grubby and dusty industry. Jesse Shirley's works would be well-screened by trees in summer, but in January, without their leaves, the trees made a less than adequate screen.

At the top of the staircase I took a bridge over the canal; and a series of terraced streets led me directly to Hanley town centre, where I was planning to take a bus. Here, a hundred and fifty years earlier, the Peace of Paris had been celebrated by the roasting of a whole ox: in those days of hard work and little leisure, any excuse for a knees-up was gratefully taken.[1]

Hanley today is a harmless enough place: there's a pleasant and unpretentious pedestrianised area, where bright shop fronts contrast with sombre deep red brick buildings; and a modern shopping centre containing a good old-fashioned covered market. Yet once Hanley was the smoky commercial heart of an area dedicated to despoiling the environment: '...roaring furnaces have opened their ponderous jaws and are belching forth volumes of smoke and liquid fire – the bowels of the earth are being dug out and converted to the requirements of the age,' commented the *Macclesfield Courier*.

As in the other pottery towns, Hanley's population increase in the eighteenth century led to squalor and depravity; but this was alleviated at intervals by spiritual revival. The established church was slow to extend its parish work to reach the irreligious masses, leaving the field free for the non-conformists, who in any case were more in tune with the independent-minded potters. The Primitive Methodists had their successes here, as did the mainstream Wesleyans, but the Kilhamites, known as the Methodist New Connexion, were particularly strong in Hanley, where the pottery manufacturer Job Ridgway helped found the Bethesda Chapel, the three thousand seater Cathedral of the Potteries.

The different strands of Methodism had their origins in bitter disagreement, but this disunity did not prevent each branch from seeing revival separately; there was enough need and spiritual hunger for them not to have to try and harvest the same corner of the field. Many other denominations also came to plant churches here, and the Church of England eventually set up missions, some of which developed into new parish churches.

When the evangelist Gipsy Smith was looking for a new post, during his time with the Salvation Army, he half-jokingly suggested to General Booth: 'Send me to the nearest place to the bottomless pit.' The General sent him to Hanley, and when the Gipsy arrived, he smelt the kiln smoke, and the sulphur from the foundries, and decided he had arrived in the right place.

---

[1] Scarratt, W (1906) *Old Times in the Potteries*

Hanley's closeness to the bottomless pit was confirmed by a bizarre and terrifying incident early in the twentieth century. Very early on a Saturday morning in December 1903, 56-year-old Thomas Holland was walking along St John Street on his way to work, as were a number of others (people generally had to work Saturdays in those days), when, as he passed number 34, the ground opened, and Thomas was swallowed up and disappeared from sight into a shaft. The witnesses had something to talk about for a long time afterwards, and thenceforward no-one could feel entirely safe even with their feet firmly on the ground.

Harmless though it seemed today, I couldn't help wondering if Hanley was actually the Nethermost Point in England: you couldn't get any lower than the nearest place to the bottomless pit. Since it was going to take so long to get to even one of the original Four Points, I wondered about calling Hanley the Nethermost Point; Scafell Pike would of course be the Uppermost Point in England, and from now on this could be the Four (plus Two) Points Ramble. Later I discovered that there is a literal Nethermost Point in England: Holme Fen in Cambridgeshire, several feet below sea level; I'll get there eventually.

It's difficult to imagine, in the twenty-first century, just how unpleasant the whole area once was. I must emphasise again, before poison pen-letters from Never-Been-So-Insulted of Hanley start arriving, that it's really quite nice nowadays; but even fifty years after the Gipsy arrived to begin his evangelism, George Orwell could still describe the Potteries with horror:

Right in among the rows of tiny blackened houses, part of the street as it were, are the 'pot banks' – conical brick chimneys like gigantic burgundy bottles buried in the soil and belching their smoke almost in your face. You come upon monstrous clay chasms hundreds of feet across and almost as deep, with little rusty tubs creeping on chain railways up one side, and on the other workmen clinging like samphire-gatherers and cutting into the face of the cliff with their picks. I passed that way in snowy weather, and even the snow was black.[1]

Gipsy Smith (left) came to Hanley as Captain Rodney Smith of the Salvation Army, a young pure-blooded Romany in his early twenties, and proved remarkably successful in communicating with ordinary working people. His particular gift was a powerful yet pleasant singing voice; he would sing hymns to entertain, but also speak to the hearts of the listeners. When he first arrived, a handful of people were meeting in the old Batty Circus, the circus ring still covered with sawdust, and when Gipsy heard them uncertainly singing 'I need Thee, Oh! I need Thee', he decided they definitely needed somebody.

[1] Orwell, G (1937) *The Road to Wigan Pier* Gollancz

I need Thee every hour, most gracious Lord;
No tender voice like Thine can peace afford.

Refrain: I need Thee, O I need Thee; every hour I need Thee;
O bless me now, my Saviour, I come to Thee.

I need Thee every hour, stay Thou nearby;
Temptations lose their power when Thou art nigh. *Refrain*

I need Thee every hour, in joy or pain;
Come quickly and abide, or life is in vain. *Refrain*

Words: Annie Hawks; tune: Robert Lowry (1872)

The work gradually built up, with the aid of open-air meetings in the Market Place, but before long Gipsy Smith was dismissed from the Salvation Army for accepting a gift. The circumstances were such that the Gipsy gained a lot of sympathy locally, and was begged to stay as a freelance evangelist. The Imperial Circus was booked, that held four thousand, and was repeatedly filled with listeners over the next four years (1882-6). The publicity that was gained by what was seen as an unfair dismissal more than compensated for the hurt; and the revival in Hanley spread to other churches: even the decorous surpliced Anglicans started holding open-air meetings, which the Gipsy regarded as a great compliment.

With detached scepticism, Arnold Bennett (right) describes a revival in Bursley in *Anna of the Five Towns*, set around the same time that Gipsy Smith was evangelising in Hanley. Musical talent is also part of the armoury of Bennett's fictional evangelist, though he is a cornettist rather than a singer; he is described as wielding 'an extraordinary histrionic gift', which is 'declamatory and full of effects carefully calculated' and exerts 'imperious hypnotism'.

Anna is moved to a blend of self-consciousness and self-disgust, quite unlike the clear conviction of sin that a real evangelist would hope for; and the old woman counselling her sees that this is not true faith or repentance. Anna wrestles with her emotions until the next morning, when forgetting to buy some bacon, and thus delaying her earthly father's breakfast, drives any thought of her heavenly Father out of her head.

As a comparison to Anna Tellwright's experience of uncertainty, compare the following exchange, when Rodney Smith himself was converted as a teenage gipsy boy:

> 'You know what you are doing?' the counsellor smiled. 'It is a great step to take, giving one's life to Jesus.'
>
> 'Well,' replied Rodney, 'I cannot trust myself for I am nothing. I cannot trust in what I have for I have nothing; and I cannot trust in what I know for I know nothing. It won't be hard for me to trust Jesus.'[1]

Bennett is good at describing suffocating human relationships, selfishness and power struggles in the family. He also excels at confused human emotions and unconscious motivation. His depiction of the revival gives an insight into false and spurious religious experience; but there is no balancing picture of the true or genuine. Presumably he believed there was no such thing.

In a short story called *Scruts*, Max Beerbohm serves up a delicious parody of Bennett's insight into the contradictions at the heart of the most ordinary personality:

> She would not try to explain, to reconcile. She abandoned herself to the exquisite mysteries of existence. And yet in her abandonment she kept a sharp look-out on herself, trying fiercely to make head or tail of her nature. She thought herself a fool. But the fact that she thought so was for her a proof of adult sapience. Odd! she gave herself up. And yet it was just by giving herself up that she seemed to glimpse sometimes her own inwardness. And these bleak revelations saddened her. But she savoured her sadness. It was the wine of life to her. And for her sadness she scorned herself, and in her conscious scorn she recovered her self-respect.
>
> It is doubtful whether the people of southern England have even yet realised how much introspection there is going on all the time in the Five Towns.[2]

As a day job, Bennett spent some time as a rent collector, like LS Lowry. Like Lowry, he kept the fact very quiet, wishing to be seen as a professional writer. No doubt the job gave him many insights into human nature, and opportunities to meet characters he might not otherwise have come into contact with. His resulting stance of detached interest and wry amusement is quite similar to Lowry's, but a little less accepting and forgiving.

I wandered round Hanley with detached interest for a little while, finding the site of the Batty Circus, close to the Market Square; but there were no Salvationists there today, and soon it was time to get a bus and head for home.

[1] Lazell, D (1970) *From the forest I came* Concordia
[2] Beerbohm, M (1912) *A Christmas Garland*

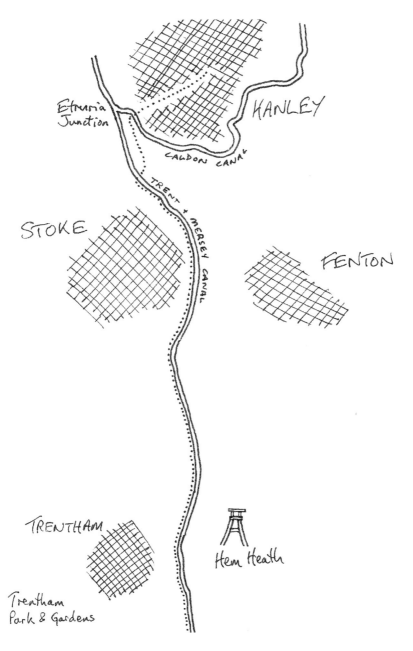

Map for chapters 11-13

Twelve: Hanley to Stoke *(1 mile)*

*Trifurcated perambulator – ancient stompers – The Towpath – explosive steam –
Shadow on the staircase – Hanley Cemetery – black ooze – purple prose – inky
water – Factory Smoke Hornpipe – late pigeon*

2nd June 2007

Two and a half years later Ishbel and I brought our friend Sylvia to the Etruria
Canal Festival, to see the visiting narrowboats, some of which were selling barge art
or rope fenders or even cheese; others showing off their painstaking restoration,
repainted into the colours of old carrying firms. The broad sweep of the first hundred
yards of the Caldon Canal was as full of life as it would have been at the first
flourishing of canal transport. A little over two hundred years earlier, the Hon. John
Byng had passed through, fancifully interpreting the scene as a willow pattern plate,
like the bone china with blue underglaze printing, that Josiah Spode II had first
perfected just a few years before:

> These intersecting canals, with their passing boats, their bridges, the
> population, the pottery ovens, and the bustle of business, remind me of a Chinese
> picture, where the angler is momentarily interrupted by a boat.[1]

Today the bustle was more of pleasure than business. Apart from narrowboats,
there were barrel organs, a big black barge horse, a working spinning wheel, wicker-

work, a mini traction
engine, birds of prey,
period-costumed Staf-
fordshire Regiment vol-
unteers, and various
canal societies.

It all made for a
lively time as we
pushed Sylvia's wheel-
chair around, though I
paid in effort for not
checking in advance
where the disabled
parking spaces were,
ending up with a steeply
roundabout and uphill
push, when I could have driven much closer. It was still worth it; we enjoyed the
spectacle and the characters such as the three-legged man in his black check trousers,
red socks and black brogues, who startled all the children with his skill in trifurcated
perambulation.

---

[1] Andrews, *op cit*

Another striking character was Ella the one-eyed Eagle Owl, who had apparently infected the other eye by scratching over-vigorously with her two-inch talons. Her huge single orange eye blazed challengingly at anyone who might contemplate accusing her of carelessness. In the same stall we watched as a little girl bravely allowed a peregrine falcon to perch on her (suitably protected) arm.

Elsewhere there were mechanical monkeys operating a barrel-organ; round the far side of the site was another barrel-organ with a human operator who was sweating profusely: 'Hard work, this, from ten till five,' he said. At least he was getting some exercise, though at £1500 the organ and £130 per tune, it was rather more expensive than gym membership.

We settled down in the marquee to listen to the Caldon Canal Stompers, a trad jazz band who played nothing post-1930, and appeared to prefer not to employ anyone born after that date either. Age had not wearied them, however, and they played their trumpet, trombone, saxophones, guitar and sousaphone with verve and enthusiasm.

The Stompers were followed by the bowler-hatted and bespectacled Andy Casserley, who played banjo, melodeon, and concertina by turns, and entertained us with old music-hall numbers such as 'I want a proper cup of coffee' (Ishbel's personal anthem), 'Where did you get that hat?' and 'When Father papered the parlour'. I hadn't heard the last song for nearly fifty years, but it must have made a deep impression once, for it floated back into my head, transformed into a slow air, maybe fifteen years after I'd heard it as an eight or nine year old on the radio. I was humming or whistling the air off and on for months before I could place where I'd heard it before. Here is the air, pitched for the A whistle:

The Towpath

111

21st March 2005

Two years earlier I'd brought Ishbel to Etruria for the first time, intending to visit the museum and then fill in the odd half-mile of the route that I hadn't walked in January. We approached on foot alongside Jesse Shirley's dusty factory, finding that it was the same firm, engaged in the same business, as had built the original bone and flint mill that forms the basis of the museum. Below us, as we came to the canal, we could see the old mill, and a party of schoolchildren on their way into the old engine house, where a beam engine is preserved for visitors to see how steam powered the mill, once water power was deemed insufficient. Erasmus Darwin was as poetically enthusiastic about the new steam technology as he was about his friend Wedgwood's revival of ancient crafts:

Nymphs! You erewhile on simmering cauldrons played,
And called delighted Savery to your aid;
Bade round the youth explosive Steam aspire
In gathering clouds, and winged the wave with fire;
Bade with cold streams the quick expansion stop,
And sunk the immense of vapour to a drop.--
Pressed by the ponderous air the Piston falls
Resistless, sliding through its iron walls;
Quick moves the balanced beam, of giant-birth,
Wields his large limbs, and nodding shakes the earth.

The Giant-Power from earth's remotest caves
Lifts with strong arm her dark reluctant waves;
Each caverned rock, and hidden den explores,
Drags her dark coals, and digs her shining ores.--
Next, in close cells of ribbed oak confined,
Gale after gale, He crowds the struggling wind;
The imprisoned storms through brazen nostrils roar,
Fan the white flame, and fuse the sparkling ore.
Here high in air the rising stream He pours
To clay-built cisterns, or to lead-lined towers;
Fresh through a thousand pipes the wave distils,
And thirsty cities drink the exuberant rills.--

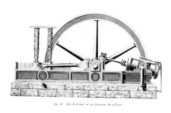

There the vast mill-stone with inebriate whirl
On trembling floors his forceful fingers twirl.
Whose flinty teeth the golden harvests grind,
Feast without blood! and nourish human-kind.

[The benevolence of the great Author of all things is greatly manifest in the sum of his works, as Dr. Balguy has well evinced in his pamphlet on Divine Benevolence asserted, printed for Davis, 1781.]

The Caldon Canal Stompers

Darwin's footnote is a reminder that, though a freethinking radical, and a great scientist, he was no atheist, but saw God's hand in all things, and considered human creativity and inventiveness to be merely a reflection of divine attributes.

To get to the museum entrance you had to cross the canal twice and double back; as we did so, the narrowboat *Challenger* was ready to leave Lock 39, a crew member winding the ground paddles down, so I leant my back against the gate to ease it open. Another boat was on the way down Lock 40, so the gate could safely be left open; and I took Ishbel up and round past the dry dock to show her the blue-handed flowerpot people, which I knew she would like. She also commented on the smartness of the garden; but the boat I had seen two months before was away cruising.

Here at Etruria lock there had been drama in 1839 as two boatmen each tried to get his narrowboat into the lock first; Bryan Bennett rammed John Carden's boat so forcefully that it sank with its load of limestone.[1]

The museum turned out not to be open for more than an hour yet – the school party must have been a special booking – so we set off to do the walk: first up the grassy slope to watch *Shadow* ascending the Bedford Street staircase locks on its way up the Caldon canal. The name, and the celtic-style uncial lettering, were familiar; but the memory of exactly where I'd seen the boat before had vanished. The lock chamber looked very deep; in fact the two steps of the staircase were of unequal heights, due to mining subsidence, the lock sides having had to be repeatedly raised.

---

[1] Hanson, H (1978) *Canal People* David & Charles

We watched the crew carefully opening the top paddles half-way, before the steersman called up that it was OK to wind them all the way up; then we headed off down a short street of Victorian terraced houses to find a way into Hanley Cemetery. There was an entrance close to the canal; and we were able to walk under tall trees alongside the water. The Cemetery itself had been largely cleared of gravestones, and had the open aspect of parkland, with wide grassy slopes and little undergrowth; room for the trees to spread themselves and for pedestrians to breathe and enjoy the spaciousness. Across the canal a derelict factory appeared to be in the process of demolition, with the exception of an isolated pair of small bottle kilns, which were presumably listed for preservation. As yet they just looked abandoned and forlorn.

The canal was quiet and empty at this early stage in the year. In its commercial heyday there would always have been loaded barges on the move:

> A trip for us was to load either coal or earthenware, in the big old-fashioned cane crates – not metal ones as they have now. Tea pots was in massive barrels, because they were bulk, and not a weighty cargo. Well, you took them down to Runcorn, and they were offloaded...then you'd ...pick up a load there, mostly of potters' materials, pebbles, stone or the white clay, everything they wanted. You'd take that up to the pot banks which were mostly on the canalside at Joyners Square, and then you'd load earthenware there and set off all over again...[1]

That round trip would have been with the black-liveried Anderton Company, later absorbed into the Mersey Weaver Ship Canal Carrying Company. Other boats passing all the year round would have been John Walley's bright boats carrying flints, or Pickford's carrying anything and everything, including, in the early years, passengers using a slower but cheaper alternative to the stage coach. In the early twentieth century one might have seen Cowburn & Cowpar's sober maroon-painted boats, specially constructed to take carbon disulphide from Manchester to Coventry.

Only hard frost or drought stopped the flow of traffic. In a long freeze such as 1947 or 1963, there was serious disruption, and great hardship among the small operators with no savings to see them through. Stoppages such as this were instrumental in the loss of traffic to other forms of transport; it seems ironic that now that we have very few hard winters, and some winters where barely a day would be cold enough to make the canal impassable, the freight is long gone. Pleasure cruising, even among the so-called 'continuous cruisers', tends to be concentrated between Easter and October.

As we drew near to the southern corner of the cemetery, and the line of railings, beyond which I had walked two months before, became more clearly visible, it seemed that there might be no convenient exit: the towpath was on the far side of the canal. But at the last moment Lock 37 came to the rescue: a little path led down to the top gate, across the gate and down the towpath under the railway, and I was standing where I had two months before. Then the pound had been dewatered, desolate and black; now it was refilled and tranquil.

---

[1] Corrie, E (1998) *Tales from the Old Inland Waterways* David & Charles

I had started the next section of the walk outside the southern edge of Hanley Cemetery, finding an alleyway leading to a footbridge over the railway. This was the main line of the North Staffordshire; not far from here, in 1846, the first sod had been turned to inaugurate the building of the line: a grand occasion, ennobled by the presence of a viscount, graced by the use of a mahogany barrow and a silver-plated spade, but rather let down when the spade buckled under the foot of John Lewis Ricardo, MP, the company chairman. One cannot imagine the practical Wedgwood using a flimsy spade, however shiny it might have been.

As I crossed the footbridge, I saw that the canal was simultaneously passing under the railway, and wondered whether there would be any access to the canal on the other side of the footbridge. At first the path looked as though it was going in entirely the wrong direction; but then it branched, and the left-hand branch curved down and round and led into the towpath beside a waterless section of canal.

The thick ooze on the canal bed was black, and all the various objects that normally lurk unseen on the bottom, and were now exposed to view, were likewise black: black bricks, black concrete slabs, black traffic cones, black bicycle tyres and dewheeled bicycle frames, and a black cash register. It wasn't pretty, but it was intriguing; and down at this level, well below the railway on one side and the A500 on the other, it was relatively quiet and peaceful.

Spoken (or rather thought) too soon: as the canal prepared to dive under a road junction, the towpath was boarded off and 'towpath closed' signs directed pedestrians up to the road. Muttering, I followed the signs onto the edge of a huge roundabout, which was in the process of radical redevelopment. No doubt it needed it; the two roundabouts on the A500 were a horrendous bottleneck for motorists. Meanwhile pedestrians were directed around and through a wilderness of roadworks, endless coils of plastic orange drainage pipes, rows of red-and-white traffic cones, towering steel piling, immense cranes in a variety of bright colours, and doubled-up queues of growling and grumbling traffic generating great gusts of carbon monoxide.

Much sooner than I had feared, a temporary wooden ramp led back down to the canal; and this stretch was in water. High walls shut out the din above, and peace and stillness rested on the water. A small buddleia bush grew out of the canal bank, its flower cones brown and bereft of butterflies in this bleak season. Although the water was brown, and the surroundings plain, it was not at all an unpleasant place to be; yet it fell short of the idyllic terms used by Thomas Bentley to describe the Trent and Mersey Canal in the prospectus issued before it was built. Since Erasmus Darwin was the literary man in the team, it has been suggested that perhaps he wrote the prospectus. But Bentley could write as well, and his marketing patter has a smoother flow and a lighter rhythm than Darwin's gorgeous bass-drum bombast. In fact Darwin took it on himself to criticise Bentley's style, and Wedgwood had to write to Bentley and soothe a bruised ego. Bentley was a salesman by nature, and knew how to appeal to investors:

And if we add the amusements of a pleasure-boat that may enable us to change the prospect, imagination can scarcely conceive the charming variety of such a landscape. Verdant lawns, waving fields of grain, pleasant groves, sequestered woods, winding streams, regular canals to different towns, orchards whose trees are bending beneath their fruit, large towns and pleasant villages, will all together present to the eye a grateful intermixture of objects, and feast the fancy with ideas equal to the most romantic illusion.[1]

Romantic illusion indeed: the late twentieth century canal cruise concept was still two hundred years in the future. The reality was rather different: hours for the boat people were long, and the life hard and dangerous. Harry Hanson lists an awesome number of hazards that killed or injured boatmen and their families: tow-ropes, windlasses and lock gates could be lethal; collisions could sink boats; even a slight bump could spill boiling water in the cabin, so scalds and burns were not uncommon; and the danger of drowning was ever-present.[2] Some of the time the boatmen might notice that they were passing through pleasant countryside, but much of their time, loading or unloading or working through locks, would be in urban surroundings, and, in the Potteries at least, these were not at all charming in the past. I was at the site of the junction with the long-vanished Newcastle-under-Lyme branch, which was not one of the cleanest in its heyday, around a hundred years after the canal opened:

> The water in it was inky black, and the stench intolerable. Large bubbles of gas were continually rising to the surface, being unmistakable proof of decomposing animal and vegetable matter. Three or four drains were running into it, and he saw the carcasses of several dogs in various stages of decomposition floating about.[3]

Also in the Victorian period, H. G. Wells, in the short story already quoted, found a savage drama in the Trent & Mersey Canal after dark, but the description was equally indicative of dreadful pollution:

> Horrocks pointed to the canal close before them now: a weird-looking place it seemed, in the blood-red reflections of the furnaces. The hot water that cooled the tuyères came into it, some fifty yards up – a tumultuous, almost boiling affluent, and the steam rose up from the water in silent white wisps and streaks, wrapping damply about them, an incessant succession of ghosts coming up from the black and red eddies, a white uprising that made the head swim.

Tom and Angela Rolt passed through in 1939, and were struck by the uniqueness of the dark townscape: the 'blackened and squat' kilns, the 'haze of steam and smoke' half-concealing the 'grimy slate roofs' and 'monstrous black slag-heaps'.

---

[1] cited in Burton, A (1989) *The Great Days of the Canals* David & Charles
[2] Hanson, 1978 *op cit*
[3] From the *Staffordshire Times*, 15 May 1875

They were able to watch the sweat-stained steelworkers going about their work right next to the water, and see working boats transporting chemicals, coal or clay: a busy scene, but a filthy one.[1]

Fresh Air from the Potteries.

The following hornpipe seems highly appropriate; either part is playable on the B flat whistle.

Factory Smoke Hornpipe

[1] Rolt, 1944, *op cit*

Maybe thirty years later still, that is, about thirty-five years ago, John Hillaby was walking this way, using the canal as part of his route from Land's End to John o' Groats. He also found it less than beautiful:

> The water that morning steamed and looked slightly iridescent. Two sad-looking swans, their under-plumage stained bright purple, cruised among bales of sodden hay and long streamers of toilet-paper.[1]

I saw nothing so off-putting, and the water merely looked a bit muddy; clearly the Potteries had cleaned up their act in recent years, even if the scene didn't approach the purple prose of Bentley. Hillaby had been planning to walk up the Caldon Canal on his way to the Derbyshire hills, but flooded towpaths, especially under bridges, forced him to abandon that plan and take to the roads, eastwards out of Hanley.

I was thankful that the weather was dry and water levels were normal. Further on, pigeons cooed under a high concrete bridge, while one of their number floated gently in the water under a smaller brick bridge close by. Its plumage was glossy and it appeared uninjured; there was no sign of decay at all; but although town pigeons are adaptable, they have not learned to breathe underwater. This one was floating face down, and had clearly turned up its toes, pegged out, and shuffled off this mortal coil. Bereft of life, defunct, departed and deceased, it was an ex-pigeon; an exanimous pigeon, to borrow a fine word from Dr Johnson's Dictionary.

[1]Hillaby, J (1970) *Journey through Britain* Paladin

Thirteen: Stoke to Barlaston *(5 miles)*

Bathroom shuffle – Stoke City – John Wain – ugly locomotive – beautiful aeroplane – nationalism – industrial icons – Mary Ann's Waltz – blunging and jiggering – black basalt – Wedgwood's knee

26th January 2005

Round the next corner, huge white letters identified the industrial premises of JONES & SHUFFLEBOTTOM LTD, who were PLUMBERS MERCHANTS and BATHROOM SPECIALISTS, and probably successful ones, judging by the scale of their operations. But would you buy a loo seat from someone called Shufflebottom? Do you get an instant impression of comfort from the name? Still, the people of the Six Towns are practical folk. Perhaps they buy the loo seat and bidet from Jones and the towel rail and shower unit from Shufflebottom.

Beyond Jones & Shuffs, a single bottle kiln stood amid picturesque dereliction, fringed with disintegrating corrugated roofs. The kiln had rounded ends and flattened sides; much mortar missing from between its brownish-yellowish bricks, and tufts of grass growing here and there where the mortar should have been. But like all the kilns, it had a beautiful shape, and I sat on a concrete slab for a couple of minutes to look at it in more detail. Steady gazing brought out the richness of the colouring of the old bricks, hardly any two the same: mustard, coffee, cinnamon or sepia, everything from yellow ochre through raw sienna to burnt umber (wonderful names from my first paintbox as a child – I liked the colours, but I liked the names even more).

Moving on again brought me to another towpath closure, necessitating another trek up to roaring traffic level and round another giant roundabout in the process of being rebuilt. However directions were plentiful and access back down to the canal was soon available. The surroundings opened out and the end of the built-up area seemed within reach. (My father, reading a draft of this chapter, commented that before the end of the walk through the Potteries he was looking forward to getting back into the country; and on foot, I was beginning to think along similar lines.)

Tranquillity would soon be regained, but there were still a few interesting memories to delve into before leaving the urban scene; it would be a shame to rush past and ignore Spode blue or Minton tiles. Minton's had several works in this area: earthenware at Eldon Place; china at Trentham Road; and tiles at Church Street. In late Georgian and early Victorian days, the well-respected Herbert Minton was the embodiment of philanthropic paternalism.

He was an outspoken opponent of the Truck system, whereby workers were paid partly in vouchers for overvalued goods; he gave a lead to his fellow employers by paying wholly in cash. He also worked to establish a fair code of practice around the 'good from oven' principle: workers on piece rates had traditionally only been paid for ware that came out of the kiln in perfect condition, and unscrupulous bosses often exploited this, rejecting substandard pots that could then be sold as seconds at great profit, since the workers had been paid nothing. Herbert Minton was totally opposed to anything that unfairly exploited the employer's advantage, such as hiring fairs timed for when trade was slack, so that workers accepted poor contracts.[1] He was much mourned when he died in 1858.

Not far away was the site of the Victoria ground, the home of Stoke City for 119 years. They're one of the oldest football clubs in England, dating back to the 1860s; they moved to the Victoria ground in 1878, and were one of the twelve founder members of the Football League ten years later. Though they seldom won the highest honours, the old ground held its memories; some very fine players were seen here, among them Gordon Banks, greatest of England goalkeepers. An even bigger legend, Stanley Matthews (left) played his last game here as a fifty-year-old. Like Port Vale, the club was once wise enough to give a manager a really extended run in the job; and Tony Waddington eventually rewarded them by guiding the club to a League Cup win at Wembley in 1972. The Victoria ground is demolished now; but we can imagine ghostly strains of 'My my my...Delilah', the fans' anthem, still floating on the breeze.

Away to my left was Fenton, the forgotten town of the Potteries; there are really Six Towns, but Arnold Bennett decided to reduce that number to five for his fictionalised version of the district, and Fenton was the one he could do without. But the town has its claims to fame: it was an engineering firm in Fenton that recognised the genius of a teenage apprentice, R. J. Mitchell, and promoted him to the drawing office. Once there he continued to impress and soon moved on to work for Supermarine, where his flair for aerodynamic design culminated in the famous Spitfire. Sadly he died of cancer before seeing the contribution his beautiful plane made to the war effort.

Over to the right were the southern slopes of Stoke, where the twentieth century novelist John Wain was born, the son of a dentist. In his autobiography, *Sprightly Running*, he writes of the alienation resulting from being seen as middle-class in an overwhelmingly working-class area. The uncertain hero of his first novel *Hurry on Down* twists and turns to avoid being forced to accept either middle-class or working-class values, and ends up with a job in the media, which he finds a niche of neutrality.

One of Wain's books that is very much rooted in the Potteries (even if much of the action takes place in London) is *The Contenders*, a fascinating study of two highly competitive, but otherwise very different, characters who each feel threatened by the other. The story is told by a common friend, non-competitive Joe Shaw, who seems to be an ordinary down-to-earth Potteries man. By the end of the book the reader is rather more interested in Joe's fate than that of either of the contenders; in fact on re-reading there are indications that the book is really about Joe all along.

Joe's comments on his own home town are typically blunt and scathing:

[1] Booth, P (1991) 'Herbert Minton' *Staffordshire Studies* Vol 3: 65-85

...that place you stop at on the way to Manchester – the one where you look out of the train window when it's slowing down, and think, 'Well, at least I don't live *here*.' ...yes, people actually do live in this place. All English towns fall into one of two categories: those that people live in because they like them, and those that people live in while they make enough money to go and live in the other kind.

...the mere fact of being brought up in a town where everything was shabby, dirty, dwarfish, peeling and generally lousy was another thing that helped to make most of us competitive. You looked round you as you stood waiting for the bus to take you to school, and you thought, 'If I don't do well I might have to end up staying *here*.'

Yet elsewhere he describes the Potteries with a love and acceptance of the industrial scene that recall Lowry's paintings or Brandt's photographs:

The dark, narrow streets, the crowded squares, the factories dotted about at random among the houses, so that you might look down any street and suddenly see a couple of kilns, looking like giant Burgundy bottles, sending out streamers of smoke only a few feet above the huddled roofs; the railway bridges, the canals, the black churches; and everywhere people scurrying about.

Joe Shaw's feelings about the Potteries – surface revulsion and underlying love – are a reflection of Wain's own ambivalence, which are an echo of Arnold Bennett's mixed feelings: he left for London and seemed to have forgotten his past, until he returned for his father's last days, and saw the possibilities of these unpretentious north midland towns.

Round another bend in the canal, two boys were feeding a big bonfire in a back yard. I assumed it was the usual bored vandalism and pyromania, until I noticed that the lads were in identical blue boiler suits, and the bonfire was in a proper incinerator cage. So they were working, presumably just out of school, and they had a task they could enjoy, for the time being. On the other side of the canal, the facade of a mostly demolished building was still standing, with bricked-up ground floor windows; this might have been all that was left of the once proud engineering firm Kerr, Stuart.

As at many other firms, the practice of pulling new apprentices' legs was traditional; here, they used to be sent to the stores for a 'long stand'. 'Right,' the storeman would say, 'I think we could give you one of those,' and he would disappear. Returning some time later, 'Was it a *long* stand you wanted?' he would inquire. 'That's right.' 'Well, you've had one now. Off you go.'

Tom Rolt, who later helped galvanise the movement to rescue England's canals from dereliction, served part of his engineering apprenticeship here; only part, because Kerr, Stuart was brought down in 1930 by a crooked chairman who had used the company's capital in another venture that had failed. The Midland bank foreclosed and destroyed, within a few weeks, what had been a healthy business with a good order book. Rolt was left with bitter memories and an aversion to harsh economic arguments.

Kerr, Stuart in Stoke dated from 1893, when the Glasgow firm took over Hartley, Arnoux & Fanning, who had been sub-contractors building steam locomotives. The tradition continued until the sudden end of the firm, with most of the engines destined for export. They were simple and rugged, intended for clients who were not likely to take much trouble over maintenance, and Kerr, Stuart locos puffed around quarries, mines and plantations in most corners of the globe. Two that were built for export to Argentina never actually went; unwanted, they were sold to the North Staffordshire, who thus acquired easily their ugliest locomotives: all the proportions are out, the frames too long for the wheelbase, the cab too big, the boiler pitched too low, the smokebox too long and the chimney perched on the *back* of it; the overall appearance jumbled and bodged. They serve to make one aware, by contrast, of the fine proportions displayed by most English locomotives.

In the distance, dead ahead, a tall modern building with an even taller chimney had me guessing whether it might be a power station or an incinerator. It turned out to be the latter, once I had covered the distance to where the canal passed close to the waste disposal works. By the towpath was erected half of a huge wheel, the pit wheel from a former mine nearby.

Up to the left was another big modern edifice, Stoke City's Britannia stadium, dating from 1997. The club battles on, sustaining its support with dreams of promotion to the top flight (recently realised), or hopes of a good cup run. Like many clubs, they sometimes have problems with a hooligan element among their supporters; doubtless just an unsavoury minority, like the BNP element in local politics, who worry some, but have not really achieved any significant breakthrough.

Probably most of the Potteries folk are too canny to be taken in by a party that preaches nationalism, yet takes its title and its colours from Britain, a union of four so different nations and cultures that it proves that differences *can* be transcended. If the English can be friends with the Welsh, with their very different culture and incomprehensible (albeit related) language, then why not with Bangladeshis, Indians, and Pakistanis, with *their* very different cultures and incomprehensible (albeit related) languages? Those who insist that immigrant cultures are alien are ignoring the fact that curry, tae-kwondo, and reggae music are far more popular among the English than haggis, shinty or Gaelic psalm-singing. No, *British* nationalism has to be reserved for the illogical and the unthinking.

Between the canal and the stadium was a pleasant tree-lined water park, which was deserted, but might well be popular in summer. Southward the Trent & Mersey now moved into an area of open fields, and seemed to have left the Potteries behind. High above, a swan flew westwards with heavy wingbeats. The towpath continued paved, as it had been all the way through Stoke: it was clearly considered a civic amenity, and even on a January weekday I met the occasional jogger or dogwalker. One little grey dog with black and white markings greeted me enthusiastically: a miniature Schnauzer.

At the canalside, above some very empty green fields, a plaque informed the curious that this had been the site of Hem Heath colliery, a working mine until comparatively recently; and that coal and ironstone had been dug locally since 1282. Apparently a huge A-frame, an icon for the local industry, had finally been demolished in 1997. It did seem curious that at a time when local authorities were paying considerable amounts to have newly-created icons erected, nobody thought of preserving one that was there ready-made.

Another canalside board advertised the Plume of Feathers, 2 miles ahead and offering food. This was very cheering news, as I would just be passing at lunchtime. On the other hand, the Four Points Ramble so far had been rich in examples of pubs that were shut at lunchtime, even ones that claimed to be open with food on offer. Accordingly, I steeled myself against disappointment, and mentally aimed to have the energy to keep walking to Stone if necessary.

Gradually the sides of the canal became urbanised again; or rather suburbanised, for this was Trentham, commuter territory, and canalside properties were clearly desirable. Some very smart narrowboats were moored by professionally-tended back gardens: *Swifdon Spirit* in blue, and *Florence*, dark green with brass trimmings. They were long boats: *Florence* in fact stretched the full width of one back garden and half of a neighbour's, and I walked a good few paces trying to guess what kind of inducement had been offered to the neighbour for mooring rights – a weekend cruise every six months? Or were they good enough friends for no formal agreement to be necessary?

In contrast to the open stretch south of the Britannia stadium, the canal was now shadowed by tall trees, some evergreen, and some ivy-clad, so that the scene was a sylvan dark green, although suburbia could be glimpsed between the tree-trunks. A fisherman sat by the water's edge; walkers strolled by; the cooing of pigeons and the squawk of moorhens mingled with the singing of numerous smaller birds. An immensely fat little wren bounced across a fight of wooden steps. Perched on the parapet of a bridge ahead was a collared dove, showing off the thin black half-circle across the nape of its neck.

27th September 2008

Not far from the shady canal was the Trentham Estate, including the famous Trentham Gardens and woodland and lakeside walks. Ishbel and I finally got round to visiting, well over three years after I had walked through Trentham.

At first Trentham appeared to be a huge park-and-shop opportunity, but beyond the many retail outlets it was finally possible to track down the Gardens and walks. Finding that the Gardens would cost us £14 between us, we decided to see if access to the woods and lakeside was cheaper; and indeed it was free, so not everything on the estate was aimed at the affluent. Together with many other less wealthy persons, we strolled in the Indian Summer sunshine, and admired the lake and the trees: huge spreading cedars and a massive four-trunked pine with long branches and long needles.

A catamaran launch ferried visitors up and down the lake; and a miniature railway transported families to the end of the lake with a frequency and slickness of service that put Network Rail to shame. A swan floated serenely in a little bay; it would not have heard the story about Trentham Lake that Josiah Wedgwood related to a young daughter, the tale of the pike that seized a swan and choked to death, drowning the swan in the process. The corpses of fish and bird were retrieved interlocked, clear proof of exactly how the double tragedy had occurred. Some

modern parents might consider the story too upsetting for a little girl; but the eighteenth century was less squeamish.

Walking back up the lakeside, we admired the fitness of the rowers: a coxed four, a pair and a single scull, all covering the water with admirable swiftness. We guessed they might be from one of the local universities. On the other side of the path a vermilion butterfly sunned itself on bramble leaves, the scalloped edge to the lower wing identifying it as a Comma – though in fact it was upside-down, so Ishbel was able to take a photo of an inverted comma, just the sort of little joke my late mother would have appreciated. Unfortunately this grayscale reproduction rather loses the glorious complementarity of vermilion on green, set off by glossy black.

26th January 2005

On my earlier walk, passing under two more bridges brought the sight of a winding hole and Trentham Lock, the first for several miles. The setting was charming: woodland on one side and fields on the other; and it was also a sign that lunch might not be far away. Passing the well-maintained Trent & Mersey mileposts at regular intervals had reassured me that I was making reasonable progress so far.

Somewhere near here, in 1839, boatman Francis Wilder had gone into a canalside field and cut some vetch with a sickle. This was nothing unusual; the boat people regarded anything that grew canalside as a sort of linear kitchen garden for their benefit, taking hay or clover for the horse, or turnips, hens, geese, sheep or deer for themselves; they might even be bold enough to milk cows that were within reach. What was less usual on this occasion was that Francis was arrested, after a struggle, by an officer of the law, and charged with the theft.[1]

On a hot, sticky, cloudy day in late summer 1939, honeymooners Tom and Angela Rolt had been at Trentham Lock, travelling north in their converted narrowboat *Cressy*, when a southbound horse-drawn barge approached, and the boatman passed on the news that Hitler had invaded Poland. Like many others at that time, the Rolts found all their plans thrown into confusion by the onset of war.

---

[1] Hanson, H (1975) *The Canal Boatmen 1760-1914* Manchester University Press

Below Trentham Lock, Bridge 104 soon came into view, where Ishbel and I had been with her mother two-and-a-half years before. This memory brought a tune to mind, which Ishbel wrote for her mother some time ago. The harmony parts were originally written separately, but we find they go reasonably well together. Paul the guitarist plays the chords with a kind of calypso rhythm.

Mary Ann's Waltz

7th September 2002

Nicholson's Guide says that 'a stop [at Bridge 104] should be on every canal traveller's itinerary', in order to see the current Wedgwood factory and visitor centre. We had taken Ishbel's mother to the Wedgwood Experience, guessing that she might like it; in fact we all did, and it made a powerful impression.

The factory was right by the canal; and near the bridge had been moored handsome narrowboats *Masquerade, War'orse* and *Swifdon Spirit;* and *Rudd*, an ugly metal box-like British Waterways barge. Across the canal a moorhen splashed water over itself, taking a thorough shower. On the other side of the bridge a heron leaned over the water, allowing us to approach quite close before stalking away across the meadow.

In the factory we wandered round watching men and women (who must have felt like animals in a zoo) doing amazingly deft and skilful things with clay or paint: processes that had satisfying, chewy, and typically English names: *blunging, jiggering, jollying, fettling.* They sounded like something out of a Harry Potter book; and indeed one of the many gifts J.K. Rowling has is minting new words that sound as if they have been in the language all along: *muggle, snidget, quaffle, flobberworm.*

The skills of the workers were also admired by Priestley, all the more when he tried to throw a pot himself and found the task beyond him:

> …the clay shot up into a frightening lop-sided tower and wobbled desperately between my hands. … the clay … could not be manipulated, indeed, could not be kept in any kind of order at all and would reach up and try to strangle me or would fling a long strand of itself at a couple of grinning lads five yards away.[1]

[1] Priestley, *op cit*

One venerable machine with a big wooden flywheel had apparently been designed by Josiah Wedgwood himself, and was still going; it hadn't worked too well when converted to electric power, so they'd reverted to the original muscle-driven design.

The exhibition section proudly displayed many different types of stoneware, bone china, porcelain and so on; Wedgwoods tried every way of competing with rival potteries for public attention. Josiah Wedgwood the founder conducted many thousands of experiments to obtain the results that he was after, and developed a variety of popular lines. Most firmly connected with the Wedgwood name were the black basalt, involving the addition of manganese, and above all the blue jasper ware, coloured with cobalt. My favourite was the basalt; unglazed, it still looked smooth as marble, yet hard as flint; Wedgwood proclaimed it 'equal in hardness to porphyry'. Erasmus Darwin praised his friend and celebrated the manufacturing processes in yet more classical verse:

Gnomes! as you now dissect with hammers fine
The granite-rock, the noduled flint calcine;
Grind with strong arm, the circling chertz betwixt,
Your pure Ka-o-lins and Pe-tun-tses mixt;
O'er each red saggars burning cave preside,
The keen-eyed Fire-Nymphs blazing by your side;
And pleased on Wedgwood ray your partial smile,
A new Etruria decks Britannia's isle.--
Charmed by your touch, the flint liquescent pours
Through finer sieves, and falls in whiter showers;
Charmed by your touch, the kneaded clay refines,
The biscuit hardens, the enamel shines;
Each nicer mould a softer feature drinks,
The bold Cameo speaks, the soft Intaglio thinks.

Wedgwood himself stood, sculpted in bronze in the courtyard with his masterpiece, the copy of the Portland Vase, and accepted being photographed with an endless stream of tourists. The statue was inaccurate in showing him with two legs, for the first of Wedgwood's Portland Vases was not produced until 1790, more than twenty years after he had had his troublesome leg amputated.

Wedgwood's knee was a curious example of misfortune that may have had beneficial effects. It was his knee stiffness that forced him to move on from the usual course of apprenticeship and apply himself instead to experimentation and innovation. It was his knee injury that precipitated his meeting with Bentley. The pain of his knee may also have had a lot to do with his constant restless activity; without that knee's problems we might never have seen blue jasper ware.

Nevertheless, he would certainly still have been a remarkable character even with a good knee and two legs all his life: his hard work, toughness, faithfulness, capacity for friendship, and persistence in experiment even after innumerable failures are all astonishing.

He understood that the essence of the scientific method is the accumulation of data through repeated experiment and analysis; and was elected to the Royal Society not for his ceramic achievements but for the Pyrometer, a far more reliable means of measuring high temperatures than any previously available, using 'the diminution of bulk while firing argillaceous bodies'.[1]

He is a sympathetic character to modern sensibility in a number of ways, one being his respect for his wife's judgment: 'I speak from experience,' he wrote, 'in female taste, without which I should have made but a poor figure amongst the Potts, not one of which of any consequence is finished without the approbation of my Sally.'

Another instance of his modern outlook was his vehement and practical opposition to the slave trade: his chained slave medallion was produced in large numbers and helped to change public opinion.

A more mundane example of what appears modern thinking can be found in the way he kept the accounts for his two factories rigidly separate: one producing cheap everyday crockery, while the other concentrated on the riskier expensive and fashionable items. He arrived at the idea of cost centres by thinking about every aspect of his business and reasoning his way to the best practice, rather than automatically doing what had been done before. Long before Henry Ford, he had organized his works on the basis of what today would be called process layout management: in effect a production line, though without sacrificing the craftsman's pride in the product.

In 1775 Wedgwood took the time to visit Land's End; and if I get that far, I shall be treading in the foot- and pegleg-steps of a great man.

[1] Thomas, *op cit*

Fourteen: Barlaston to Stone *(3 miles)*

Culpeper dives deep – IPA – Concrete sheep – redwing pie – Lord St Vincent's Hornpipe – non-stop station – Bold Benjamin – unpopular baby – famous old ale unavailable – Bull & Bear reunion – The Happy Meeting – lively little sea port

26th January 2005

As I passed Bridge 104 again, two and a half years later, I saw only a small cruiser, *Sally Ann* from Milford Haven, and wondered whether she had come all the way by water. Road seemed more likely for at least some of the journey; she was small enough to be towed by an ordinary car. Finally approaching the Plume of

Feathers, I saw *Nuphar Lutea*, a long green narrowboat, moored on the far bank; and ignorantly wondered what the name might mean. Was it one of those disguised puns, *Hiphar Lutin* or *Knot Phor Sail*, that cause sensitive passers-by to groan? But I couldn't make it into anything. Later I found that *Nuphar lutea* is the botanical name for the Yellow Water-lily, also known as the Brandy Bottle from the smell of the flowers and the shape of the seed head. Culpeper, in the *English Physician and Family Dispensatory,* says 'they are cold and dry, and stop lust: I never dived so deep to find what virtue the roots have.' Yet by the time of the *English Physician Enlarged,* he must have done some deep diving, for he is able to give much more information:

> …the leaves do cool all inflammations, both outward and inward heat of agues; and so do the flowers also, either by the syrup or conserve; the syrup helps much to procure rest, and to settle the brain of frantic persons, by cooling the hot distemperature of the head. The seed as well as the root is effectual to stay fluxes of blood or humours, either of wounds or of the belly; but the roots are most used, and more effectual to cool, bind, and restrain all fluxes in man or woman. The root is likewise very good for those whose urine is hot and sharp, to be boiled in wine or water, and the decoction drank.

You could remember that, when you next feel frantic and in need of a brain-settler. Finding the Plume of Feathers open and serving food meant that I was in no need of water-lily syrup, but could order tuna mayo baguette and some Greene King IPA. The barrel was new, and the handpump coughed and frothed so that the beer took a long time to settle. I sat in an armchair and looked around as I waited for it. The pub had been very recently done up, using a lot of chunky wood, not in imitation of traditional style, but just using wood because it's a wonderful substance to look at. Was it gazing at wood grain that first gave map-makers the idea for contour lines? Silver trophies were displayed here and there, presumably for bowling, since the pub had a green. Comfortable armchairs were a very practical touch.

The baguette was a very good size and the beer excellent. Greene King here was a long way north-west of its origins in Bury St Edmunds, but I wasn't grumbling. 'An easy-drinking, amber-coloured session bitter,' says CAMRA of IPA, 'bitterness predominates throughout, leading to a somewhat astringent finish'. The beer connoisseurs are less impressed with the way Greene King take over other local and regional real ale producers, and close them down soon afterwards. In recent years Morland, Ruddles, Hardy's & Hanson's, and Ridley's, have all been acquired and had their breweries closed; beer may still appear with those names, but it isn't brewed where it used to be. Yet Greene King itself is undeniably good beer. I stretched out my legs and tried to make the most of an unusually relaxing lunchbreak; but eventually it was time to get on my feet again.

The broad paved towpath, which had made for good progress and easy walking, ended at Bridge 103 by Barlaston. It became a narrow path in the middle of a broad grassy bank, well-mown for some way beyond the bridge; this was clearly a desirable property area. Little terraces of tiny old cottages were smartly done up and tastefully embellished, and flanked by weeping willows, beautiful in outline even in this leafless season. And beyond the terraces was a palatial detached property with not only its own boat – plain in dark primer, in the process of maintenance – but its own wharf arm, with room for two full-length narrowboats. Beyond the wharf, concrete sheep, smartly painted in natural colours, stood in grazing attitudes on the back lawn.

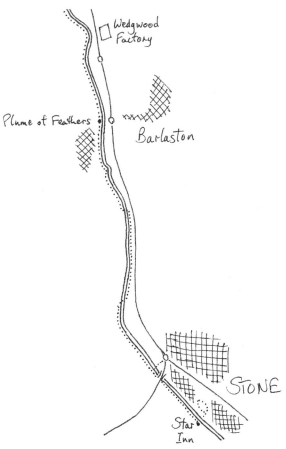

Map for chapter 14

Richard Dean's historical map of the *Canals of North Staffordshire*[1] marks this spot as the Barlaston Dockyard, so presumably the wharf arm was restored rather than constructed from scratch. But still, what wonderful one-up-manship; how to stop your friends feeling proud of their fine double garages – show them round your own mini-marina.

Gradually the towpath became muddier; as the canal curved towards the next bridge, reeds and rushes fringed both banks, the beginnings of new green pushing vigorously through the limp pale yellow of last year's leaves. A heron flew heavily over towards the Trent, neck doubled and legs trailing. Before long the towpath mud was dictating a somewhat zigzag course to avoid the softest and wettest parts.

A thrush hopped through the bare branches of an elder tree; then the red patches under the wings showed it to be a redwing, though it was unusual to see one completely on its own. Usually they come over from Scandinavia in flocks, if the weather there is cold. Bewick notes that the Redwing is also known as the Swinepipe, or Wind Thrush, and that it makes good eating:

...the Romans held them in such estimation that they kept thousands of them together in aviaries, and fed them with a sort of paste made of bruised figs and flour... these aviaries were so contrived as to admit light barely sufficient to direct them to their food; every object which might tend to remind them of their former liberty was carefully kept out of sight, such as the fields, the woods, the birds, or whatever might disturb the repose necessary to their improvement. Under this management these birds fattened, to the great profit of their proprietors, who sold them to Roman epicures for three denarii, or about two shillings sterling each.[2]

How would they have been eaten? In a pie, like blackbirds? As I asked myself this question, a four-coach diesel multiple-unit droned by on the other side of the canal. It occurred to me that that might have been the 13.35 from Stone to Stoke, which I would possibly have caught if I hadn't stopped for lunch. But I was aiming for the 15.05 (I'd checked the times on the internet the night before), and there was plenty of time to catch that.

As a ten-year-old trainspotter, I hated the new DMUs. Carriages moving by themselves, what was the point of that? As far as I was concerned, railways existed to give steam locomotives something to do, so motorised carriages were a total abomination. In those days, I could at least wait for the next train, since that might well be steam-hauled. In 2005, I needed imagination to conjure up a sturdy North Staffordshire tank engine chuffing northwards with its local stopping train.

---

[1] which I had bought at the stall at Bosley bottom lock, two and a half years earlier (see chapter 5)
[2] Bewick, *op cit*

.Bridge 100 turned out to be a roving bridge, taking the towpath over to the other side, where it became much drier and grassier, leading on to the mellow green-grown redbrick Bridge 99, beyond which was a quiet reach shaded by tall grey-skinned beeches and glossy rhododendron. A wren fluttered here and there among the beech roots by the water's edge. I realised that I must have walked past Meaford Power Station without noticing it at all – not that there was any problem with that – but either it had been very well screened by trees, or the muddiness of the towpath at that point had fixed my eyes firmly downwards.

Below the beeches was Lock 34, the top of a flight of four at Meaford. These were built in 1810 to replace the original 1772 staircase of three. The site of the vanished staircase could be seen by Lock 33, though you wouldn't notice anything if you didn't know where to look. Another roving bridge took the towpath back to the right-hand side, but not to the same muddy state. The last two closely-spaced locks brought the canal into open space, bounded by a very new and rather upmarket (double garages all over the place) housing estate, which made the most of its canal frontage, and had some long smart narrowboats moored by its well-mown lawns. *Catkin, Covenant Connection,* and *Kassel* lay in fortuitously alliterative juxtaposition, waiting to float their owners away from hectic lifestyles or hefty mortgages. Not far from the towpath side of the canal was a rather noisy main road, but where it came closest a little clump of newly-planted saplings promised to form a screen eventually. Meanwhile a flock of long-tailed tits twittered among the tiny branches.

Following in the horse's hoofprints of the Honourable John Byng, who came this way when the canal was barely twenty years old, I was fortunate not to encounter such wet weather: 'As the rain now returned with violence,' he wrote, 'I trotted briskly along, by the side of the navigation to the end of the town of Stone; where I re-hovel'd for an hour' – by which he meant that he sheltered in some wayside shed in the vain hope that the rain might stop.

Stone takes its name from 'stanes', referring to the cairn that was raised in the seventh century to mark the martyrdom of Rufin and Wulfad, the sons of Wulfhere, Lord of Mercia. They had become Christians, like their mother Ermenilda; their father, however, had them hunted and killed. Wulfhere had himself once professed Christianity, but returned to the pagan faith of his father Penda once he realized the necessary change of heart involved in living as a Christian; and he was determined that his sons would not follow this shocking new faith. Such implacable opposition to a young person *choosing* what to believe, rather than having it chosen for them, is still found in the twenty-first century: a young man was baptized in our church the other day who had been thrown out of the family home the very day he told his parents of his Christian faith.

Stone became a market town in 1251, but remained small and unimportant for centuries. In the eighteenth century it developed some significance as a coaching town: up to 38 coaches a day passed through, and inns multiplied to cater for travellers' needs, but few stayed longer than they had to.

One famous local boy was John Jervis, who left the town at the age of thirteen to pursue a career in the navy, though he came from a landlocked county that at that date had virtually no navigable water of any kind. Nevertheless Jervis (left) eventually became a highly respected admiral, and gained a title in 1797 by winning the great battle of Cape St Vincent, together with his brilliant young subordinate, Horatio Nelson. Jervis, the veteran of forty years of sea battles, led his line of ships between two groups of Spanish vessels, enabling his gunners to fire into both enemy lines at once. Nelson understood and supported his admiral's tactics, and a crushing victory was won. Jervis became an earl, and the following fine hornpipe was probably composed in his honour.

Lord St Vincent's Hornpipe

The next bridge marked the spot where Ishbel and I had once walked nearly two years before. The narrowboats moored here were different, however: *Heart of Gold, Azalea,* and *Ilford*, all colourfully painted, and the last still in the form of a traditional working boat with tarpaulins stretched over a central beam. By the next lock a footpath led the short distance to Stone station.

The station was in good condition, its architecture still showing a strong North Staffordshire influence in the three Jacobean-style gables and the tall stone finials above. It was designed in 1848 by HA Hunt, who was also responsible for Stoke station. Stone station was originally built in a V-shape, with straight platforms on the line southwards to Colwich, and sharply-curved platforms veering away south-west towards Stafford. In the late twentieth century the straight platforms were removed, although both lines remain well used.

A timetable by the station entrance confirmed the next train was at 1505, as I'd seen on the internet the night before. Reassuringly, the timetable was only a month old, and valid for two more months. Trying to enter the station building to buy a ticket, however, only proved that all doors were locked. A window gave a view of a business meeting in progress, and the truth dawned that the building had been sold off to a private company, while only the platforms and a bleak shelter remained for the travelling public.

.It was all clean and in good order, so I crossed the footbridge and settled down to wait, playing a few tunes on the whistle since there was nobody else there to be offended by the odd bum note. A couple of times a 4-coach diesel multiple unit droned through without stopping; in the good old days that might have been a smart 0-6-4 tank in NSR madder lake livery – though the train would certainly have stopped. Occasionally a high speed train whined past on the Colwich line, bound eventually for London; that might once have been a Royal Scot, resplendent in LMS red; or earlier, a Claughton in LNWR blackberry black. The 1505 seemed to be rather late, but that wasn't particularly surprising, and I didn't start to worry until about 1530. Of course at an unstaffed station there was no way to get information on delays or cancellations; and it would have been irritating to walk off just as the train finally appeared. All the same, I was close to giving up, when a chap in a suit appeared on the other platform – presumably an employee of the tenants of the building – and called 'You're not waiting for a train, are you?'

I said I was, mentioning the internet and the noticeboard outside. 'The internet's wrong,' came the reply. 'It's all a cock-up. There haven't been any trains stopping here since last summer. I thought you were trainspotting.'

Trainspotting? With nothing to see but utterly boring diesel multiple units? I summoned up the grace to thank the guy for letting me know about the true state of affairs, and trudged off, eventually to find a bus and arrive home an hour and a half later than I had promised Ishbel. What a way to run the country: a railway line in current use, and a station still in good enough order to be usable, and no trains that actually deign to stop – all because one set of politicians dug themselves out of a financial hole by selling the family silver (as Lord Stockton put it) to companies with no interest in providing a service and every interest in lining their shareholders' pockets; and then another set of politicians took no interest in tackling a difficult problem, and every interest in manipulating their public image by tackling little problems that provide photo-opportunities.

5th *May 2003*

Nearly two years earlier, I had walked the canal towpath through Stone with Ishbel in the late afternoon of the first May Bank Holiday; mild and sunny, excellent walking weather. Emerging from the shadow of Bridge 96, I was startled to see a railway signalbox in a canalside garden; and even more startled to see the nameplate: Stoneycombe Sidings Signal Box. So the box had come hundreds of miles from a quarry near my hometown in Devon. The garden also boasted two ex-Great Western lower quadrant signals: there was definitely a passionate rail enthusiast here.

We strolled on, past extensive factory buildings – reasonably neat and tidy and partly screened from the canal by willow trees – until we came to Newcastle Road Lock, where there was a very fine garden of ornamental shrubs beyond the far side of the lock; and then a narrow brick-lined tunnel to take the barge horses under the main road.

Emerging from the tunnel, we found ourselves at Stone Wharf, busy with boatyards, chandler's, and many moored narrowboats. As always some had feminine names: *Eva, Ariadne, Ina* and *Christina*; others had wildlife names: *Otter, Elderflower, Mandarin* and *Mr Mole Too*; and other names were intriguing: *Delphinus* and *Hubberholme*. We watched *Completely Foxed* swinging carefully round and backing into the narrow dock at Trunk Wharf; the wharf's name dated from when the Trent & Mersey Canal carried Brindley's original name, the Grand Trunk Canal; and the canal company's head office had been here in Stone. *Pro Patriam Populumque Fluit*, 'it flows for the nation and the people', was a grandiose and yet accurate motto: everyone benefited from the Grand Trunk.

Stone in particular gained from the Grand Trunk Canal; in 1788, Shaw 'the Topographer' wrote:

> ...in a few years after [the canal] was finished, I saw the smile of hope brighten every countenance; the value of manufactures arise in the most unthought of places; new buildings and new streets spring up in many parts of Staffordshire, where it passes; the poor no longer starving on the bread of poverty; and the rich grow greatly richer. The market town of Stone in particular soon felt this comfortable change; which from a poor insignificant place is now grown neat and handsome in its buildings, and from its wharfs and busy traffic, wears the lively aspect of a little sea port.

I'd been at this wharf before, in the spring of 1985, on another of Chris Parker's week-long barge trips: the Four Counties Ring this time. We'd hired *Ben Gunn* from Staffordshire Narrowboats at Stone Wharf. Eighteen years on, I hardly recognised the place – something was missing. There was extensive redevelopment under way near the bridge, so maybe the scene I was trying to recall had disappeared to make room for the new construction. The trip on *Ben Gunn* was generally quite hazy in memory, though I did recall the baby crying in the night. It was the first time – and I pray the last – that I had been on a week's cruise where someone had decided to bring along a baby to enjoy the trip. The infant was fine, no trouble and quite entertaining – during the day.

The name *Ben Gunn* had put me in mind of a sea song I had recently learned:

> Brave Admiral Cole he's gone to sea, oh me boys oh!
> Brave Admiral Cole he's gone to sea, oh!
> Brave Admiral Cole he's gone to sea,
> Along of our ship's company,
> On board the bold *Benjamin*, oh!

Some of the verses had a highly ominous ring to them:

> We sailed out five hundred men, oh me boys oh!
> We sailed out five hundred men, oh!
> We sailed out five hundred men,
> And brought back but sixty-one.
> They were lost in bold *Benjamin*, oh!

During the week I'd whiled away odd moments in adapting verses of the old song for our own trip, verses which remained in my head, unsung in order to spare feelings:

> Here's the baby crying half the night, oh me boys oh!
> Here's the baby crying half the night, oh!
> Here's the baby crying half the night,
> And what the crew muttered was hardly polite:
> They would ha' dropped it off the bold *Benjamin Gunn*, oh!

Of course, everybody had pretended they didn't really mind being kept awake after an energetic day's lock-wheeling, paddle-winding and gate-pushing; the infant hadn't actually been asked to crawl the plank; and presumably by 2003, as I tried to recall the trip long before, was either on a gap year in Patagonia or the Philippines, or well into his first year at university.

.Stone Wharf was where Tom Rolt's converted narrowboat *Cressy* was condemned and left to rot in 1951, ending twelve years of life afloat. It had been a lifestyle that appealed to many, though few then had the means and will to try it. Half a century later, many are living the same dream; and their boats should stay afloat longer, as greater experience of converted boats ensures avoidance of the lack of ventilation between floorboards and keel that was *Cressy's* fatal design fault.

Across the canal was a fine curving gabled warehouse, inscribed 'Joule's Stone Ale' in huge letters, together with squat red crosses on a green background. Joule's rang no bells with me, but you can find out anything on the internet. It seems that the brewing family in Stone were cousins of the Joule who gave his name to the unit of energy, and who had such a high regard for physics as a field of enquiry: 'It is evident,' he wrote, 'that an acquaintance with natural laws means no less than an acquaintance with the mind of God therein expressed'.[1]

The Joules in Stone had been brewing since the mid-eighteenth century, at which time they took over the King's Arms Brewery, claimed to be the oldest in the country, dating from the early seventeenth century. Joule's Brewery prospered: their premier product, 'Stone Ale', used to travel by barge up to Ashton-under-Lyne, and even became internationally famous. In 1887 the San Francisco Chronicle remarked: 'the quality of this famous old English ale, so long and favourably known to that market, is today the same as it was twenty-five years ago, and is to be found as a favourite in many of the English alehouses in town'.

In the twentieth century their beer won medals or awards in seven different years between 1919 and 1957, but that did not prevent (more likely it encouraged) Charrington's takeover in 1970. Brewing ceased within five years; an event typical of the period before the Campaign for Real Ale gained enough momentum to show the big corporations that the customers' views were worth taking into account. No way remained of finding out what Joule's tasted like.

Another former product of the inventive town of Stone was Hovis, whose factory we walked past many miles earlier in Macclesfield. The originator of the recipe was the miller Richard Smith of Stone in 1885, who first marketed Hovis under the less iconic and more mundane brand name of 'Smith's Patent Germ Bread'.

We strolled on, past the high brick walls adorned with their short-armed red crosses (the green background was necessary to avoid confusion with the Red Cross organisation), until we came to Star Lock, sandwiched between a smart restaurant and a historic pub, which both made the most of their lockside location. A medium-sized narrowboat, *Henry V*, was on its way up, allowing drinkers and diners alike to observe the unhurried action. The pub, the Star Inn, apparently had thirteen rooms with no two on the same level, though I didn't find this out until afterwards. The excellence of Banks' bitter made up to some extent for the extinction of Joule's.

A walk through the town centre took us past the Crown, where Josiah Wedgwood was elected Treasurer of the Grand Trunk Canal in 1766. A generation later the

---

[1] cited in Blanchard, J (2000) *Does God believe in atheists?* Evangelical Press

136

Hon. John Byng stayed there after his rain-soaked ride from Trentham, and was pleased to find the Crown

> ...a good house, with symptoms of civility, where, taking possession of a good parlour (with a good fire, June 29th!) I ordered dinner, and then read the London newspapers, with great avidity, after my *long* ride. – I was much entertained from my window, with the sight of 4 lusty Irish gentlemen coming forth from a hackney post chaise with 4 horses; and afterwards being repacked in another; instead of going in two chaises, drawn by 2 horses each; which I should have thought a pleasanter way of travelling.[1]

Then as now, the Irish preferred company and the *craic* to English notions of peace and comfort. The Crown still looked a fine inn in the 21st century. However, we failed to locate another historic pub I had read about: the Bull & Bear, where the converted slave trader John Newton (right) was reunited with his wife Mary in the autumn of 1755. John, having given up captaining slave ships, had been working as Tide Surveyor in Liverpool; Mary had been recuperating in London after a serious illness. Now she was well enough to travel, and John could not bear to wait in Liverpool, but came to meet her at a coaching inn on the way. As they rested in the Bull & Bear, they talked and planned, and resolved

> ...to declare God's goodness together, not merely in secret or to each other, but by the whole course of our lives; to love Him more than we love each other; and to commit to Him our dearest concerns, and in every trouble to go to Him who has so often heard our prayers and done us good.[2]

The Happy Meeting

---

[1] Andrews, *op cit*

[2] cited in Davidson, N (1997) *How Sweet the Sound* Ambassador

The Four Points Ramble route is intended to pass Olney, where Newton lived as neighbour to William Cowper the poet, and collaborated in hymnwriting so creatively and lastingly; but that is still some way in the future, for Newton as for ourselves. Here is one of his fine hymns, set to a Staffordshire melody:

Tune: Thomas Butts, 1754

Though troubles assail and dangers affright,
Though friends should all fail and foes all unite,
Yet one thing secures us, whatever betide,
The promise assures us, "The Lord will provide."

The birds, without barn or storehouse, are fed;
From them let us learn to trust for our bread.
His saints what is fitting shall ne'er be denied
So long as 'tis written, "The Lord will provide."

No strength of our own, nor goodness we claim;
Yet, since we have known the Saviour's great Name,
In this our strong tower for safety we hide:
Almighty His power, "The Lord will provide."

Cheddleton Flint Mill

Conclusion

Having walked and written three books, I still hadn't reached Lichfield. On reaching Stone, more than two and a half years after beginning the project, I had come 145 miles from Gargrave, the starting point of Book One, and written not far off 1,000 words a mile. At that rate, the entire Four Points Ramble would require over two million words. It would not be wise to look ahead in those terms: one day's walk at a time, a couple of pages writing at a time.

The early parts of this third book were walked in quite disjointed order, and it was sometimes difficult to weld chapters together as continuous text; but the later sections were walked more or less in order, which made things easier, and the route has coalesced in memory as a continuous path all the way from Gargrave.

Some cumulative totals were more impressive than the meagre miles-so-far. Since Gargrave I had walked alongside seven canals (Leeds & Liverpool, Rochdale, Huddersfield Narrow, Peak Forest, Macclesfield, Caldon, and Trent & Mersey), all of them open and in cruising use; encountered the lines of seven pre-grouping railway companies (Midland, Great Northern, Lancashire & Yorkshire, London & North-Western, Great Central, Cheshire Lines, and North Staffordshire), and sampled thirteen local or regional beers (Tetley's, Thwaites', Timothy Taylor's, Lees', Greenfield, Robinson's, Hyde's, Banks's, Greenall's, Marston's, Boddington's, Theakston's, and Greene King).

The 54-mile route of Book Three had taken me over four high points: Sponds Hill, at 1347 feet, the Saddle of Kerridge, at about 940 feet (the path didn't lead over the highest end of the hill), Tegg's Nose, at about 1240 feet, and The Cloud, at 1125 feet. After The Cloud, it was downhill most of the way.

Writing took more time than walking, but was still enjoyable, in a different sort of way. The approach must have been influenced to some extent by many other travel books: particular inspirations in my youth were Hilaire Belloc's *The Path to Rome*, and Robert Louis Stevenson's *Travels with a Donkey*. But I think one of the strongest influences and inspirations has been decades of listening to Test Match Special on the radio, with its genial characters burbling on about anything and everything, and using acute observation and accurate description of telling detail to set the scene for the listener.

A prime example, almost a kind of writer's motto, is the line I heard many years ago (possibly around 1966), delivered with the weighty deep-chested West Country emphasis so characteristic of John Arlott:

'A small piece of *paper* is blowing along the ground near square *leg*.'

139

Bibliography

Andrews, CB ed (1934) *The Torrington Diaries* Eyre & Spottiswoode
Bennett, A (1902) *Anna of the Five Towns*
Bennett, A (1908) *The Old Wives' Tale*
Bennett, A (1910) *Clayhanger*
Bennett, A (1911) *The Card*
Bewick, T (1826) *A History of British Birds*
Blanchard, J (2000) *Does God believe in atheists?* Evangelical Press
Bode, H (2ed 1980) *James Brindley* Shire
Bolton, D (1990) *Race against Time* Methuen
Booth, P (1991) 'Herbert Minton' *Staffordshire Studies* Vol 3: 65-85
Brailsford, D (1978) *Reminiscences of the Knotty* NSR Co Ltd
Burton, A (1989) *The Great Days of the Canals* David & Charles
Chaplin, T (2ed 1989) *Narrow Boats* Whittet Books
Cheatle, JRW (1976) *A Guide to the British Landscape* Collins
Cheshire County Council (1986) *Rail, Water & Tramways*
Christiansen, R (1997) *Portrait of the North Staffordshire Railway* Ian Allan
Corrie, E (1998) *Tales from the Old Inland Waterways* David & Charles
Culpeper, N (1653) *The Complete Herbal*
Davidson, N (1997) *How Sweet the Sound* Ambassador
Davies, CS (1961) *A History of Macclesfield* Manchester University Press
Essery, T (1996) *Steam Locomotives Compared* Atlantic
Falkus, H (1980) *Nature Detective* Penguin
Farrar, KE ed (1903) *Letters of Josiah Wedgwood*
Fisher, J (1967) *Thorburn's Birds* Ebury Press
Gasson, H (2005) 'The greatest engine ever built at Swindon' *Steam World*, June 2005
Gooders, J & Boyer, T (1986) *Ducks of Britain* Dragon's World
Grindon, LH (1882) *Country Rambles* Palmer & Howe: Manchester
Hanson, H (1975) *The Canal Boatmen 1760-1914* Manchester University Press
Hanson, H (1978) *Canal People* David & Charles
Hillaby, J (1970) *Journey through Britain* Paladin
Hoskins, WG (1955) *The Making of the English Landscape* Hodder & Stoughton
Jeuda, B (1980) *The Leek, Caldon & Waterhouses Railway* NSR Co Ltd
Jeuda, B (1999) *The Churnet Valley Railway* Lightmoor Press
Lazell, D (1970) *From the forest I came* Concordia
Lewis, RA (1969) *Staffordshire Waterways* Staffordshire Education QLS
Meteyard, E (1866) *Life of Josiah Wedgwood*
Mitford, MR (1824-32) *Our Village*
Morris, Rev FO (1850) *British Birds*
Morris, W (1877) *The Lesser Arts*
Morris, W (1881) *Some Hints on Pattern-Designing*
Oddie, W (2ed 1995) *Little Black Bird Book* Robson
Orwell, G (1937) *The Road to Wigan Pier* Gollancz
Reilly, R (1992) *Josiah Wedgwood* Macmillan
Richards, R (1957) *The Manor of Gawsworth* Ancient Monuments Society
Rolt, LTC (2ed 1948) *Narrow Boat* Eyre & Spottiswoode

Rolt, LTC (1977) *Landscape with Canals* Alan Sutton
Scarratt, W (1906) *Old Times in the Potteries*
Suleman, D (1993) *On the Level* North Cheshire Cruising Club
Thomas, J (1971) *The Rise of the Staffordshire Potteries* Adams & Dart
Uglow, J (2002) *The Lunar Men* Faber & Faber
Wain, J (1953) *Hurry on Down* Secker & Warburg
Wain, J (1958) *The Contenders* Macmillan
Wain, J (1962) *Sprightly Running* Macmillan
Warrillow, EJD (1952) *History of Etruria* Etruscan Publications
Warrillow, EJD (1960) *A Sociological History of Stoke-on-Trent* Etruscan Publications
Wells, HG (1895) 'The Cone' *Unicorn,* September 18, 1895.

The Caldon Canal

The Beneficiary Charities

On these two pages are details of the four charities that will benefit from the sale of this book.

Registered Charity No 259766

  The Caldon Canal was classed as a remainder waterway in 1968. This meant that British Waterways were not bound to maintain the canal to a navigable standard. Eventually an agreement was reached between Stafford County Council, Stoke on Trent City Council and British Waterways Board to restore the canal.Thus in 1974 the Caldon Canal was reopened at a cost of £100,000. Following the reopening of the Canal in 1974, the Caldon Society's aim was to have the Caldon upgraded to cruising status and this was finally achieved in 1983.

  During these years the Society had been active not only in its campaigning but with its volunteers who cleared obstructions, vegetation and removed debris. A feasibility study has recently reported on the possibility of returning the canal to Leek. In 2004 the Society changed its name to the Caldon and Uttoxeter Trust as it wished to investigate the possibility of restoring the Uttoxeter Canal from Froghall through the magnificent Churnet Valley, all the way to Uttoxeter. The Trust was instrumental in the restoration of the canal basin at Froghall, the first part of the project.

  Members of the Society meet regularly with other Canal user groups, the IWA, British Waterways and Local Authorities as well as maintaining links with other interested organizations. *More details on* www.cuct.org.uk

Campaign to Protect
Rural England - Cheshire

Registered charity number 1089685.

  We are the champions of England's countryside and we welcome the support of all who care about it. CPRE is a registered charity with over 60,000 members and supporters living in our cities, towns, villages and the countryside. We operate as a network with over 200 district groups, a branch in every county, a group in every region and a National Office. Over 2,000 parish councils and 800 amenity societies belong to CPRE. This makes CPRE a powerful combination of effective local action and strong national campaigning.

We are one of the longest established and most respected environmental groups, influencing policy and raising awareness ever since we were founded in 1926.

More details on www.cprecheshire.org.uk

tearfund

Registered Charity No 265464

Tearfund is a Christian relief and development agency working with a global network of local churches to help eradicate poverty. Our ten-year vision is to see 50 million people released from material and spiritual poverty through a worldwide network of 100,000 local churches.

Two words that can clear a room fastest?

Global poverty.

At Tearfund we have a vision: the local church working at its best - loving its neighbour both right on the doorstep and where love's needed most. Making connections across the world between the people with resources and the people who desperately need them. Letting people here at home be part of a miracle, a miracle that sees people in poverty at last able to make real changes.

(picture:Andrew from Fombe village, Malawi. Photo: Marcus Perkins/Tearfund – used by permission (www.tearfund.org)

Lives are being transformed. Today, through our work, this is a reality - this is the miracle we're witnessing. *'There is a lot of help by NGOs but the poorest of the poor are not spotted. You really have to go down to the ground to find the poorest who have no voice in the village. We found that churches work with everyone – and they know who are the poorest people in the village.'* (Cuthbert Gondwe, Tearfund partner, Malawi)

DMH
Douglas Macmillan Hospice

Registered Charity Number: 1071613

The Hospice is the only adult Hospice for the people of **North Staffordshire** and surrounding villages. We were established in 1973 and have grown over the years not only in size but also in the range and amount of care services available for local people.

Our consultant led multi-disciplinary clinical team provide specialist palliative care for people facing cancer and other life-limiting illnesses; and help and support for their families and carers.

We do not charge for the care and help we provide, we rely on voluntary donations and some statutory funding to meet our running and development costs.

Our team of nurses, doctors, healthcare assistants, volunteers, chaplains, social workers, therapists, and support staff care for all the needs of our patients facing a terminal illness: physical, emotional, social and spiritual. Together we aim to help patients both at home and in the Hospice to achieve the very best quality of life, whatever their life expectancy, days, weeks or months.

More details on www.dmhospice.org.uk

Path near Danes Moss

Arthur ca 1993 - 2008 R.J.P.